Series/Number 07-163

MULTIPLE CORRESPONDENCE ANALYSIS

Brigitte Le Roux

Université Paris Descartes

Henry Rouanet

Université Paris Descartes

Los Angeles | London | New Delhi
Singapore | Washington DC

For information:

 SAGE Publications, Inc.
2455 Teller Road
Thousand Oaks,
    California 91320
E-mail: order@sagepub.com

SAGE Publications Ltd.
1 Oliver's Yard
55 City Road, London,
    EC1Y 1SP
United Kingdom

SAGE Publications India Pvt. Ltd.
B 1/I 1 Mohan Cooperative
    Industrial Area
Mathura Road, New Delhi 110 044
India

SAGE Publications Asia-Pacific
    Pte. Ltd.
33 Pekin Street #02-01
Far East Square
Singapore 048763

Printed in the United States of America

Library of Congress Cataloging-in-Publication Data

Le Roux, Brigitte.
Multiple correspondence analysis/Brigitte Le Roux, Henry Rouanet.
    p. cm.—(Quantitative applications in the social sciences; 163)
ISBN 978-1-4129-6897-3 (alk. paper)
    1. Correspondence analysis (Statistics) 2. Multiple comparisons (Statistics)
I. Rouanet, Henry. II. Title.

QA278.5.L4 2010
519.5′37—dc22   2009075095

This book is printed on acid-free paper.

09   10   11   12   13   10   9   8   7   6   5   4   3   2   1

Acquisitions Editor:	Vicki Knight
Associate Editor:	Lauren Habib
Editorial Assistant:	Ashley Dodd
Production Editor:	Brittany Bauhaus
Copy Editor:	QuADS Prepress (P) Ltd.
Typesetter:	C&M Digitals (P) Ltd.
Proofreader:	Jenifer Kooiman
Cover Designer:	Candice Harman
Marketing Manager:	Stephanie Adams

012210/m8

CONTENTS

ABOUT THE AUTHORS

Brigitte Le Roux is Maître de Conférences at the Laboratoire de Mathématiques Appliquées (MAP5), CNRS (the French National Center for Scientific Research) Université Paris Descartes and associate researcher at the political research center of Sciences–Po Paris (CEVIPOF/CNRS). She is an assistant director for the journal *Mathématiques & Sciences Humaines,* and she serves on the editorial board of the journal *Actes de la Recherche en Sciences Sociales.* She completed her doctoral dissertation with Jean-Paul Benzécri in 1970 at the Faculté des Sciences de Paris. She has contributed to numerous theoretical research works and full-scale empirical studies involving geometric data analysis.

   Web site: www.mi.parisdescartes.fr/~lerb

Henry Rouanet was a research assistant of Patrick Suppes at the Center for Mathematical Studies in Social Sciences of Stanford University, from 1960 to 1962. Then he was the head of the "Mathematics and Psychology Group," a research unit of CNRS. He ended his career as a guest researcher at the Laboratoire d'Informatique de l'Université Paris Descartes (LIPADE). Analysis of variance and its Bayesian extensions were his major research interests. The bulk of this monograph was written during the last year of his life.

   Web site: www.mi.parisdescartes.fr/~rouanet

   The authors have written numerous articles and several books on statistics and geometric data analysis.

SERIES EDITOR'S INTRODUCTION

Correspondence analysis is a descriptive method for examining relationships among categorical variables. It is a close analogue of principal component analysis for quantitative variables.

Correspondence analysis has been developed in several locations, under several names, by several individuals—including, in 1940 by R. A. Fisher, a pivotal figure in the history of statistics during the first half of the 20th century. It was the French statistician Jean-Paul Benzécri, however, who developed and popularized the method in the 1960s and 1970s, first in France, and then more generally in Europe, and who gave it its now widely used name (analyse des correspondances).

Simple correspondence analysis, as developed, for example, by Fisher, examines the relationship between two variables in a contingency table. As in principal component analysis, where the general goal is to approximate relationships among variables in a space of reduced dimension, the general goal of correspondence analysis is to closely reproduce the similarities among the rows and among the columns of the table in a space of low dimension. That is, for example, rows that are close in the space have similar conditional distributions across the columns of the table.

Multiple correspondence analysis, the subject of the current monograph by Brigitte Le Roux and Henry Rouanet, extends this essential idea to several categorical variables. In multiple correspondence analysis, the object is to display geometrically the rows and columns of the data table—where rows represent individuals and columns the categories of the variables—in a low-dimensional space, so that proximity in the space indicates similarity of categories and of individuals. In sociology, multiple correspondence analysis has figured prominently in the work of Pierre Bourdieu.

Le Roux and Rouanet present a thorough introduction to multiple correspondence analysis, beginning with the geometric ideas that underlie the method. By emphasizing the geometry, and explaining its relationship to the linear algebra of multiple correspondence analysis, the authors provide an accessible, intuitive approach to the subject, without entangling the reader in a maze of matrix decompositions. Le Roux and Rouanet's approach to multiple correspondence stresses the geometric examination of

viii

individuals as an inductive (or essentially descriptive) method, including focusing on subgroups of individuals who are differentiated with respect to certain variables not used directly in a multiple correspondence analysis—a process that they term "structured data analysis" of "supplementary variables."

It is my hope and expectation that this monograph will help extend the application of multiple correspondence analysis, particularly in North America.

Editor's note: This is the first monograph to appear under my editorship of the QASS series. It was begun under the direction of the previous series editor, Tim Futing Liao.

—John Fox
Series Editor

ACKNOWLEDGMENTS

Many have contributed to the development of this monograph. Special thanks to Philippe Bonnet (Université Paris Descartes), Frédéric Lebaron (Université de Picardie), and Johs Hjellbrekke (University of Bergen, Norway) for their extremely useful comments, encouraging advice, and fruitful reading of the proofs.

We wish to thank Jean Chiche and Pascal Perrineau (CNRS/ Institut de Sciences Politiques de Paris), François Denord and Julien Duval (CNRS, Paris), Louis-André Vallet (CREST, Paris), Geneviève Vincent (Université Paris Descartes), Donald Broady and Mikael Börjesson (Uppsala University), Mike Savage and Alan Warde (Manchester University, UK), and Olav Korsnes (University of Bergen), who all have assisted us in the diffusion of geometric data analysis.

We are grateful to the graduate students of the Research Master's degree of Sciences–Po (Paris) with whom we have tested many previous versions of this monograph.

Our gratitude and recognition goes to the PhD students and the researchers who attended the autumn schools at Uppsala University (2006, 2007) and those who attended the summer school at the Centre de Sociologie Européenne in Paris (2007), and also to the PhD students of the course in Copenhagen University (2009) who were the first to be exposed to the (almost) final version.

We would like to thank Tim Liao, Vicki Knight, and John Fox, editors at Sage, and their three anonymous reviewers, for their valuable comments in the process of preparing this monograph.

The authors gratefully acknowledge the help and encouragement of Patrick Suppes (Stanford University) and, above all, they wish to recall the constructive support of Pierre Bourdieu, to whom this book is a posthumous homage.

CHAPTER 1. INTRODUCTION

Between quantity and quality there is geometry.

The purpose of this monograph is to provide a nontechnical introduction to multiple correspondence analysis (MCA) as a method in its own right; no prior knowledge of correspondence analysis (CA) is needed. The presentation will be practically oriented and with the needs of research in mind: gathering relevant data, formulating questions of interest, and linking statistical interpretation to geometric representations. The procedures will be presented in detail using a real example, stressing the unique capacity of MCA to handle full-scale research studies.

Plan of Chapter 1. We introduce MCA as one of the main paradigms of geometric data analysis (GDA) (Section 1.1). We summarize historical landmarks (Section 1.2). We briefly present statistical data analysis in Bourdieu's work (Section 1.3). We introduce our leading example (Section 1.4). We review methodological points (Section 1.5). Last, we present the organization of the book (Section 1.6).

1.1 MCA as a Geometric Method

The three key ideas in GDA. In the 1960s, J.-P. Benzécri initiated a statistical approach around the CA method. We designate this statistical approach,[1] including the analysis of structured data and its inductive extensions, *geometric data analysis*.

The three key ideas are the following ones:

1. *Geometric modeling.* Starting with a two-way table, the elements of the two sets indexing the entries of the table become points in a geometric space, defining two *clouds of points*. For an Individuals × Categorical Variables table, we have the scheme shown in Figure 1.1 (p. 2).

2. *Formal approach.* The methods are based on the mathematical theory of linear algebra. As Benzécri once put it: "All in all, data analysis, in

---

[1] This approach is known in French as "Analyse des Données." In English, "Data Analysis"— the literal translation of "Analyse des Données"—does not sound precise enough. The phrase *geometric data analysis* was suggested to us in 1996 by Patrick Suppes (Stanford University).

1

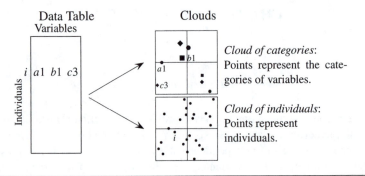

Figure 1.1 Data table and the two clouds of points generated by MCA.

good mathematics, is simply searching for eigenvectors; all the science (or the art) of it is just finding the right matrix to diagonalize."[2]

3. *Description first!* Geometric modeling comes before probabilistic modeling, in the spirit of *inductive philosophy*: "The model should follow the data, not the reverse!" The basic outcomes of geometric methods are *descriptive statistics*, in the technical sense that they do not depend on the size of the data set. For instance, in Individuals × Variables tables, if the individual observations are duplicated, the clouds of points are unchanged (see Le Roux & Rouanet, 2004, p. 299).

Three paradigms of GDA. (1) For two-way frequency tables, CA is directly applicable. For Individuals × Variables tables, there are two other GDA paradigms available. (2) For numerical variables, there is *principal component analysis* (PCA), a classical multivariate method recast as a GDA method, that is, for which the basic space is that of individuals (see Rouanet, 2006, p. 139). (3) For categorical variables, there is MCA.

Individuals may be people, or "statistical individuals," such as cases, firms, items, experimental units, time periods, and so on. Categories may result from the pooling of qualitative or quantitative variables. In the literature, categories are also called *modalities*.

1.2 Historical Landmarks

In his historical survey[3] of multivariate statistics, Benzécri (1982) makes due reference to precursor papers: to Fisher (1940) and Guttman (1941) on

---

[2] The formal approach is developed in Le Roux and Rouanet (2004).

[3] A summary of Benzécri's survey is found in Murtagh (2005, pp. 1–9).

optimal scaling, and Burt (1950) on *factor analysis*. He also refers to the *quantification method* developed by Hayashi (1952), and to what is known today as *multidimensional scaling* (MDS) developed by Shepard (1962). What clearly emerges from this survey is that the geometric modeling of data brought about an in-depth renewal in the field of multivariate statistics.

The history of GDA can be divided into three periods (landmark years are given as a guide).

- *First period: Emergence (1963–1973)*

The core of CA was established in 1963 and soon combined with clustering methods (see, e.g., Benzécri, 1969). "Analyse des Données" was established with the two volumes by Benzécri et al. (1973) (*Taxinomie* and *Analyse des correspondances*). Meanwhile, statistics textbooks incorporating CA began to appear, such as the one by Lebart and Fénelon (1971), followed by many others, all written in French.

- *Second period: Splendid isolation (1973–1980)*

GDA was used widely in France where it was applied to all sorts of data sets. MCA, as the counterpart of PCA for categorical variables, became standard for the analysis of questionnaires. The phrase *analyse des correspondances multiples* appeared for the first time in Lebart (1975). Developments in the method, both theoretical and applied, were published mostly in *Cahiers d'Analyse des Données* (from 1976 onward).

- *Third period: International recognition (since 1981)*

Books in English that directly stemmed from the work done in France were published: Greenacre (1984), Lebart, Morineau, and Warwick (1984), Benzécri (1992), Le Roux and Rouanet (2004), and Murtagh (2005). The Gifi group, much aware of the works of the French school, has published many articles on MCA—which it calls "homogeneity analysis"—see Gifi (1990). Introductory books on CA began to appear: Weller and Romney (1990), Greenacre (1993), Clausen (1998), and so on.

Where do we stand now? The phrase *correspondence analysis* is well accepted in English. The basic procedures of GDA can be found in statistical software used worldwide. Conferences specifically devoted to "CA and related methods" have been organized outside France: in Cologne (1991, 1995, 1999), Barcelona (2003), and Rotterdam (2007). However, in the field of multivariate statistics, geometric methods remain rather isolated. For MCA, the situation is really poor. This method, which is so powerful for analyzing full-scale research studies, is still rarely discussed and therefore is underused.

To sum up, CA is now recognized and used, but GDA as a whole methodology, and MCA in particular, are waiting to be discovered by a wider audience.

1.3 Bourdieu and Statistical Data Analysis

It is a commonplace to speak of correspondence analysis as "Bourdieu's statistical method": rightly so, since Bourdieu's work has provided an exemplary use of CA. In fact, beyond CA, statistical data analysis has been a constant concern for Bourdieu. Hereafter, we briefly outline Bourdieu's shift from traditional statistics to multiple correspondence analysis.

• *First period (1960s and early 1970s): Traditional statistics*

As early as the "Algerian times" (1958–1961), Bourdieu cooperated with INSEE statisticians (the French national institute of official statistics). In this first period, Bourdieu's writings are filled with contingency tables and chi-squares.

• *Second period (mid-1970s): Correspondence analysis*

In the early 1970s, Bourdieu elaborated the concept of field; at the same time he was becoming aware of the shortcomings of traditional statistical tools:

> The particular relations between a dependent variable (political opinion) and so-called independent variables such as sex, age and religion, tend to dissimulate the complete system of relations that make up the true principle of the force and form specific to the effects recorded in such and such particular correlation. (Bourdieu, in *La Distinction*, 1979, p. 103)

Meanwhile, the geometric approach was developing around correspondence analysis. Bourdieu turned to the new method, applying it to Individuals × Questions tables, which enabled him to synthesize a host of contingency tables by the two clouds: that of categories (in Bourdieu's words, "properties") and that of individuals (see Bourdieu and Saint-Martin, 1976; *La Distinction*, 1979):[4]

---

[4] See Rouanet, Ackermann, and Le Roux (2000). This paper was read at the Conference on the *Empirical Investigation of Social Space* organized by J. Blasius and H. Rouanet and held in Cologne (October 7–9, 1998) with Bourdieu's participation.

I use Correspondence Analysis very much, because I think that it is essentially a relational procedure whose philosophy fully expresses what in my view constitutes social reality. It is a procedure that 'thinks' in relations, as I try to do it with the concept of field. (Preface of the German edition of *Le Métier de Sociologue*, 1991)

- *Third period (from the late 1970s): Multiple correspondence analysis*

In the late 1970s, MCA definitely became the preferred method used by Bourdieu and his school: *Homo Academicus, Noblesse d'Etat, Structures sociales de l'économie*, etc. In 2001, in his last lecture at the Collège de France, Bourdieu emphasized again that

Those who know the principles of multiple correspondence analysis will grasp the affinities between this method of mathematical analysis and the thinking in terms of field. (in *Science de la science et réflexivité*, p. 70, 2001)

1.4 The Taste Example

The Taste Example, which is inspired by Bourdieu's work, will be the leading example in this book; it will be taken up again in detail from Section 3 onward. It is drawn from the data used in the paper by Le Roux, Rouanet, Savage, and Warde (2008) on lifestyle in the United Kingdom.

For teaching purposes, we have restricted ourselves to four questions pertaining to *taste*, with 29 response categories, and to the 1215 individuals who answered the four questions, choosing one category per question.

- *Preferred TV program* (8 categories): news, comedy, police, nature, sport, films, drama, soap operas;
- *Preferred Film* (8 categories): action, comedy, costume drama, documentary, horror, musical, romance, SciFi;
- *Preferred type of Art* (7 categories): performance, landscape, renaissance, still life, portrait, modern, impressionism;
- *Preferred place to Eat out* (6 categories): fish & chips, pub, Indian restaurant, Italian restaurant, French restaurant, steak house.

From Data Table to Clouds

Hereafter are shown extracts of the Individuals × Questions table (Table 1.1, p. 6), and the two clouds (produced by MCA) projected onto

Table 1.1 *Taste Example.* Extract from the Individuals × Questions table.

	TV	Film	Art	Eat out
1	Soap	Action	Landscape	SteakHouse
⋮	⋮	⋮	⋮	⋮
7	News	Action	Landscape	IndianRest
⋮	⋮	⋮	⋮	⋮
31	Soap	Romance	Portrait	Fish&Chips
⋮	⋮	⋮	⋮	⋮
235	News	Costume Drama	Renaissance	FrenchRest
⋮	⋮	⋮	⋮	⋮
679	Comedy	Horror	Modern	Indian
⋮	⋮	⋮	⋮	⋮
1215	Soap	Documentary	Landscape	SteakHouse

Note: A row corresponds to the *response pattern* of an individual. For instance, the pattern of individual #235 is (*TV*–News, *Film*–Costume Drama, *Art*–Renaissance, *Eat out*–FrenchRest).

the first principal plane: the cloud of *categories* (Figure 1.2, p. 7) and the cloud of *individuals* (Figure 1.3, p. 8).[5]

First Comments on the Clouds

Cloud of categories. On the left of Figure 1.2 (p. 7), we find "matter-of-fact" tastes and established values, whereas on the right, we find tastes oriented toward "fiction worlds," with an opposition between "popular" (top) and "sophisticated" (bottom).

Cloud of individuals. In Figure 1.3 (p. 8), points represent individuals;[6] the location of an individual reflects the 4 responses of this individual. For instance, individual #31 is in the top-right corner, as are the 4 categories chosen by this individual (see Table 1.1, Figures 1.2 and 1.3).

The distance between individual points reflects the dissimilarities between response patterns of individuals. Individuals who choose the same four categories are represented by points at the same location. For instance, there are 12 individuals giving the same responses as individual #7, therefore they share the same location, hence the large size of the point in

---

[5] Color versions of some figures are available on the first author's Web site.

[6] Locate yourself on the figure! To do so use the computer program "locate_yourself," be found on the first author's Web site.

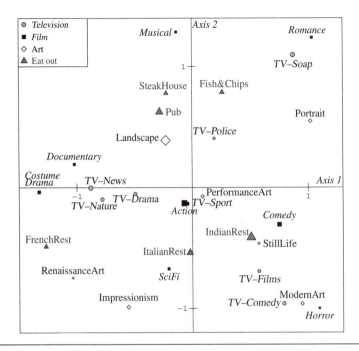

Figure 1.2 *Taste Example.* Cloud of the 29 categories of the four questions in Principal plane 1-2.

Figure 1.3. In contrast, individuals #31 and #235, who have very different tastes (Table 1.1, p. 6), are represented by remote points.

Further Comments

Distances. A cloud of points is not a simple "graphical display," like a temperature chart; a cloud of points is like a geographic map with the *same distance scale in all directions*. A geometric diagram cannot be stretched or shrunk along one particular dimension. For instance, the distance in the plane between individuals #235 and #1215 is slightly greater than the distance between individuals #7 and #679. If for graphical purposes the diagram is enlarged, the distance ratios should be unchanged. Note that the two clouds, in Figures 1.2 and 1.3, are on the same distance scale.

Dimensionality. A basic characteristic of a cloud of points is its dimensionality. The simplest case is a *one-dimensional* cloud, whose points lie on a *line*. Then comes a *two-dimensional* cloud, whose points lie in a *plane*,

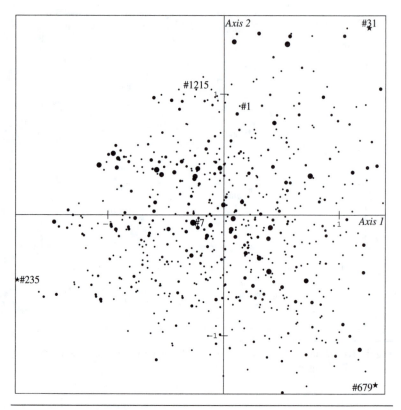

Figure 1.3 *Taste Example.* Cloud of 1215 individuals with landmark individuals(★) in principal plane 1-2.

then a three-dimensional cloud, and so on. In MCA, the clouds of categories and of individuals have the same dimensionality, which is usually very high. The full clouds are referred to their principal axes 1, 2, 3... ranked in decreasing order of importance. The clouds of Figures 1.2 and 1.3 are actually the projections of the full clouds onto the plane of the principal axes 1 and 2, that is, onto the principal plane 1-2. Two axes may not suffice for interpretation, as will be seen for the Taste Example later in the book (see Section 3, p. 51).

Aids to Interpretation

Contributions.   The contribution of point to axis is a statistic that depends both on the distance from the point to the origin point along the axis and on the weight of the point. The contributions of points to axes are the main *aid to interpretation*.

Supplementary elements. The construction of the clouds is based on 1215 individuals, called *active individuals*, and on 4 variables, called *active variables*. Once the clouds are constructed, *supplementary individuals* may be put into the study and placed in the cloud of individuals. Similarly, *supplementary variables* may be added and their categories can be placed in the cloud of categories. Supplementary elements considerably enrich the interpretation of data (see Section 3, pp. 58–60).

Toward Structured Data Analysis. Data can be analyzed further by focusing on *subclouds of individuals*. For instance, two subclouds of individuals, that correspond to extreme age groups, are shown in Figure 1.4. The investigation of individual differences will be developed in Section 4.

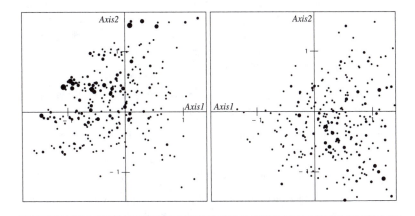

Figure 1.4 *Taste Example.* Two subclouds of individuals corresponding to over = 55 (left) and 18–34 (right) age groups, in principal plane 1-2 (compared to Figure 1.3 the size of this figure has been halved [half size]).

Steps of the analysis of a data set

The process of analyzing data with MCA can be conducted in nine steps.

1. Preparation of the data table for MCA: Choose active individuals and active variables and encode categories.

2. Elementary statistical analyses.

3. Proceeding to MCA: The basic results of the analysis are eigenvalues and coordinates, then contributions and clouds. A first examination of the contributions (points with conspicuously dominating contributions, etc.) will be made.

4. Informal inspection of the clouds in several principal planes, at least in plane 1-2, to check the forms of the clouds, looking for indices that point to a lack of homogeneity (isolated groups of points, stratified clouds, etc.). This inspection of clouds may lead to revising the analysis: choice of active variables and/or individuals, modification of codings (feedback loop).

5. *Interpretation.* Decide how many axes need to be interpreted, using eigenvalues and modified rates. Interpret axes in the cloud of categories, using contributions. As Benzécri teaches us:

> Interpreting an axis amounts to finding out what is similar, on the one hand, between all the elements figuring on the right of the origin and, on the other hand, between all that is written on the left; and expressing with conciseness and precision the contrast (or opposition) between the two extremes. (Benzécri, 1992, p. 405)

It may be convenient, at the price of some oversimplification, to qualify the sides of each axis with a short label.

6. Inspecting and "dressing up" the cloud of individuals (shape, landmark patterns).

7. Supplementary elements: individuals and variables.

8. Deep investigation of the cloud of individuals (structuring factors and concentration ellipses, between–within variances ...).

9. Statistical inference.

The steps of MCA will be conveyed by means of the Taste Example in Section 3 (Steps 1–8), Section 4 (Step 9), and Section 5 (Step 10).

1.5 Methodological Points

Frame model. Any empirical study involves the statement of a frame model, which guides the collection of data and the interpretation of results. In GDA, two principles should be followed (see Benzécri, 1992, pp. 382–383; Benzécri et al., 1973, p. 21).

1. *Homogeneity*: The theme of the study delimits the domain for collecting data, that is, individuals and variables. When there are both qualitative and quantitative variables, homogeneity can be achieved by *preliminary coding*. By viewing each variable as a question with response categories, we end up with a quasi-universal coding format: the questionnaire.

2. *Exhaustiveness*: Individuals, as well as variables, should constitute an exhaustive or at least representative inventory of the domain under study.

The frame model should serve as a reminder that GDA methods, like all statistical methods, can only be fruitful if they deal with *relevant data*. Performing a geometric analysis does *not* mean gathering disparate data and looking for "what comes out" of the computer. On the other hand, in GDA there is no drastic *parsimony* principle of the kind required in regression methods. MCA is eminently apt at revealing the structural complexities of tables with a large number of variables, as it synthesizes a host of analyses of two-way tables (Variable × Variable). On this point, with only 4 questions, the Taste Example is certainly not an exhaustive data set of lifestyle in the United Kingdom: It is a compromise between a mere illustration and a real case study and is only meant to present the techniques of MCA.

Domains of application.   Since its emergence in France, MCA has been applied in a large range of domains: social sciences, epidemiology, market research, satisfaction surveys, etc.

In the social sciences, GDA has given rise to a statistical practice in sharp contrast with the conventional practice based on numerical indicators (regression coefficients, etc.) and the *star system* (* significant at .05 level, ** significant at .01, etc.). This contrast reflects two conceptions of the statistical tool, namely, sustaining a *sociology of variables* versus constructing a *social space*. The "elective affinities" between social field and geometric representations led Bourdieu to use CA, then MCA, consistently from the late 1970s.

Clustering.   The concern for clustering—putting together objects that go together—is most natural. Guided by spatial intuition, researchers in front of a cloud of points spontaneously draw contours around clusters.

Efficient methods of clustering, such as ascending hierarchical clustering (AHC) methods, yield systems of nested partitions of the kind encountered in natural sciences. The AHC method applied to a cloud of points with the *variance criterion* is in harmony with geometric structures. For Benzécri (1992), it is the "companion method of CA."

Frequently Asked Questions. While the outstanding capacity of GDA methods to reveal underlying structures is well recognized today, the following two questions are frequently raised:

1. Are geometric methods amenable to statistical inference?

2. Can they be used for explanatory purposes?

The answer to both questions is "Yes, definitely."

1. The real question about statistical inference is when and how to use it in a fruitful way. In the inductive philosophy, inference procedures should be used in an attempt to extend descriptive conclusions of interest. Thus, when the geometric analysis brings out a clear-cut opposition on an axis between two subclouds of individuals (say, between young and elderly people), the researcher's recurrent query must be faced: "Is the observed difference a genuine one, or might it have occurred by chance?" As we will see (Section 5), procedures such as test values and confidence zones convincingly answer such queries. The golden rule is that inference procedures should always be subordinate to substantive conclusions. Thus, the model of data, already enriched by structured data analysis, will be further substantiated by inductive data analysis, in accordance with the following scheme.

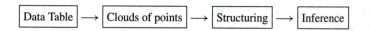

2. When explanatory phraseology is used in connection with statistical procedures ("explanatory variable" vs. "variable to be explained," etc.), it can be confusing. The elongation of a metallic bar can be regressed on temperature, or temperature can be regressed on the elongation of the bar. Whereas, explanatory assertions are clear enough in the framework of a substantive theory external to statistics; for instance, in the expansion theory in physics, temperature explains the elongation of a metallic bar, not the reverse. It is wise to hold the position that statistics per se does not explain anything, but that all sorts of statistical methods can be used to substantiate explanatory theories, as the case may be.

1.6 Organization of the Monograph

Mathematical prerequisites. High school geometry (mathematical formulas are kept to a minimum and are illustrated on examples). Matrix formulas appear in a separate section.

Statistical prerequisites. Elementary descriptive procedures; mean, variance; scatter diagrams, simple linear regression, correlation, contingency tables.

Outline of Subsequent Chapters

Chapter 2: The basic geometry of a cloud of points is presented.

Chapter 3: The MCA method is presented, and the steps of analysis are described in detail on the Taste Example, with a guide to interpretation.

Chapter 4: The investigation of the cloud of individuals is pursued with the analysis of structured data, providing a link with classical methods such as analysis of variance.

Chapter 5: Inductive data analysis is outlined; the useful inference procedures of test values and confidence ellipses are presented.

Chapter 6: We quickly review two full-scale research studies using MCA.

Appendix: We present a symbol index, matrix formulas, and a note on software.

CHAPTER 2. THE GEOMETRY OF
A CLOUD OF POINTS

Geometric objects can be described by numbers;
they are not reducible to numbers.

The essence of GDA methods is to construct *clouds of points*. Once a cloud is constructed, whatever the particular GDA method it originates from, its study can be conducted along the same lines. This is why this section is devoted to the geometry of a cloud of points. The underlying mathematical theory is *multidimensional geometry*, which is the extension of elementary geometry to a *geometric space* with more than three dimensions. Formally, a cloud of points is a finite set of points in a geometric space. In fact, to introduce the geometry of a cloud of points, elementary geometry will suffice.[1]

Plan of Chapter 2. We first recall basic geometric notions (Section 2.1). We introduce the cloud of points with a two-dimensional cloud and define mean point and variance (Section 2.2). We discuss subclouds, partition of a cloud, and contributions (Sections 2.3 and 2.4). We introduce principal axes and principal clouds (Section 2.5). We sketch the extension to higher-dimensional clouds (Section 2.6). Then we present computation formulas for a plane cloud (Section 2.7).

2.1 Basic Geometric Notions

The elements of a geometric space are *points*. Two distinct points determine a *line* (one-dimensional subspace); three nonaligned points determine a *plane* (two-dimensional subspace). Points will be denoted by roman capital letters: M, P, A, and so on. With a pair of points (P,M), there is associated a geometric *vector* denoted by $\overrightarrow{PM}$, or M − P ("terminal minus initial"), as the *deviation* from P to M.

The concept of vector is *directed*; that is, $\overrightarrow{MP} = -\overrightarrow{PM}$. If point M coincides with point P, the associated vector $\overrightarrow{PM}$ (or $\overrightarrow{MP}$) is the *null vector*, denoted by $\overrightarrow{0}$. A directed line is called an *axis*. The notions of a geometric space are of two sorts: affine and metric.

---

[1] At this point, readers may wish to refresh their high school geometry; or just skim this section at the first reading of the book. For a presentation of clouds of points based on linear algebra, see Le Roux and Rouanet (2004, chap. 10).

- *Affine* notions pertain to alignment, direction, and barycenter. The basic affine operation is the sum of vectors, using the *parallelogram rule*:

$$\overrightarrow{PM} + \overrightarrow{PN} = \overrightarrow{PQ}$$

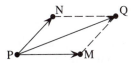

Barycenter of 2 points. Let (A, B) be a pair of points with respective weights (a, b) (with $a > 0$ and $b > 0$); the barycenter of (A, B) is by definition the point G of segment AB such that $a\,\overrightarrow{GA} = -b\,\overrightarrow{GB}$ (figure with $a = 3, b = 2$).

Property. If P is any point in the space, then

$$\overrightarrow{PG} = \frac{a}{a+b}\,\overrightarrow{PA} + \frac{b}{a+b}\,\overrightarrow{PB},$$

that is, $\overrightarrow{PG}$ is the weighted average of vectors $(\overrightarrow{PA}, \overrightarrow{PB})$.

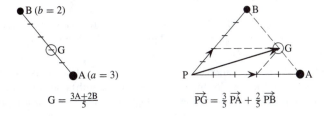

$$G = \frac{3A+2B}{5} \qquad\qquad \overrightarrow{PG} = \tfrac{3}{5}\,\overrightarrow{PA} + \tfrac{2}{5}\,\overrightarrow{PB}$$

These properties lead to conceptualizing the barycenter as a *weighted average of points*, writing

$$G = \frac{aA + bB}{a+b}.$$

If the two weights are equal, the barycenter is the *midpoint* of the segment.

The following table summarizes the basic operations on numbers, vectors and points, and their outcomes. Observe that vectors can be added, but *not* points.

	Adding	Subtracting	Averaging
Numbers	number	number	number
Vectors	vector	vector	vector
Points	[*not defined*]	vector (deviation)	point (barycenter)

- *Metric* notions pertain to *distances* and *angles*, especially right angles. The *distance* between two points M and P is called the length of segment MP (or PM) and denoted by MP (or PM). The distance is symmetric and verifies the *triangle inequality* $PQ \leq PM + MQ$, with $PQ = PM + MQ$ if and only if point M lies on segment PQ between P and Q. Once a unit length is fixed, distances can be expressed by nonnegative numbers.

The fundamental metric property is the *Pythagorean theorem*: If $\overrightarrow{PM}$ and $\overrightarrow{MQ}$ are perpendicular (triangle MPQ with right angle at M), then

$$(PM)^2 + (MQ)^2 = (PQ)^2.$$

2.2 Cloud of Points

The Target Example

Ready-made clouds of points occur when observations are points recorded in the ambient physical space. We will present the basic geometry of a cloud on the *Target Example*, a cloud of 10 points in a plane (thinking of the points as impacts on a target). Taking the natural Euclidean distance in the plane, we will choose a distance unit (i.e., unit length) and refer the plane to rectangular axes (horizontal and vertical) crossing at the origin point O (target center) as shown in Figure 2.1 (p. 17).

Points versus numbers. One goes "from points to numbers" by taking the coordinates of each point—here the "*initial coordinates*"—relative to the axes. The 10 abscissas $(x_1^i)_{i=1,2,\ldots10}$ and ordinates $(x_2^i)_{i=1,2,\ldots10}$ of the points of the cloud define the coordinate variables x_1 and x_2, called "*initial variables*" (Table 2.1, p. 17). Conversely, starting with a couple of numbers taken as coordinates, one goes "from numbers to points" by constructing the points from the coordinates.

The geometric notions (mean point, sum of squares, variance) readily extend those pertaining to numerical variables.

Target Example. The means of the initial variables are $\bar{x}_1 = (0 + 6 + \ldots + 12)/10 = 6$ and $\bar{x}_2 = 0$. The variances are $v_1 = \big((0 - 6)^2 + (6 - 6)^2 + \cdots + (12 - 6)^2\big)/10 = 40$ and $v_2 = 52$. Observe that the initial variables

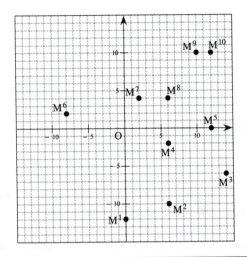

Figure 2.1 *Target Example.*Cloud of 10 points with origin point O, initial axes, and unit length.

are *correlated*; their covariance is $c = \Big((0-6) \times (-12-0) + \ldots + (12-6) \times (10-0) \Big)/10 = +8$. Hence, the correlation $r = +8/\sqrt{40 \times 52} = +0.175$.

Table 2.1 Initial coordinates of 10 points.

	x_1	x_2
M^1	0	−12
M^2	6	−10
M^3	14	−6
M^4	6	−2
M^5	12	0
M^6	−8	2
M^7	2	4
M^8	6	4
M^9	10	10
M^{10}	12	10
Means	6	0
Variances	40	52
Covariance |	+8	

Note on the variance formula

1. In GDA—as in the great statistical books by Kendall and Stuart (1973), Cramér (1946), and so on—for a sample as well as for a population, the variance is defined by dividing the sum of squares by n (total number of observations), not by $n - 1$.

2. The term *inertia* (borrowed from mechanics) is also used as a synonym of variance.

Note on orthogonality. In this book, the term orthogonality will be reserved for *geometric* orthogonality (e.g., perpendicular axes), as opposed to statistical noncorrelation (sometimes called "orthogonality" too).

Mean point of a cloud. *Definition*: If P is any point in the space and if the n points of the cloud are denoted by $(M^i)_{i=1,2,\ldots n}$, the mean point of the cloud is the terminal point G of the vector $\overrightarrow{PG} = \sum \overrightarrow{PM^i}\,/n$. The mean point G does not depend on the choice of point P.

If we replace P by the mean point G, we get the *barycentric property*:

$$\frac{1}{n}\sum \overrightarrow{GM^i} = \overrightarrow{0},$$

that is, the mean of the deviations from the mean point to the points of the cloud is the null vector.

These properties lead to writing

$$G = \sum M^i/n$$

expressing that point G is properly the mean (i.e., average) of the points of the cloud.

Property. The coordinates of G are the means of the coordinate variables.

Target Example. Letting $P = O$, $\overrightarrow{OG} = (\overrightarrow{OM^1} + \overrightarrow{OM^2} + \cdots + \overrightarrow{OM^{10}})/10$; G has coordinates $(\overline{x}_1, \overline{x}_2) = (6, 0)$.

Distances between points. In rectangular axes, the squared distance between two points is, by the Pythagorean theorem, equal to the sum of the two squared distances along the axes.

Target Example. The squared distance between the two points M^1 and M^2 is $6^2 + 2^2 = 40$ (Figure 2.1, p. 17), hence the distance $M^1M^2 = \sqrt{40} = 6.32$.

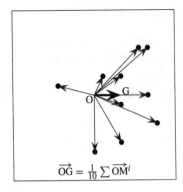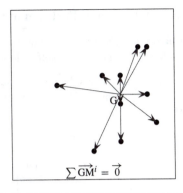

$$\overrightarrow{OG} = \tfrac{1}{10}\sum \overrightarrow{OM^i}$$

$$\sum \overrightarrow{GM^i} = \vec{0}$$

Figure 2.2 *Target Example.* Mean point and barycentric property.

Variance of a cloud. *Definition*: The *variance of a cloud* is the mean of the squared distances from the points of the cloud to the mean point (see Benzécri, 1992, p. 93). The *standard deviation of the cloud* is the square root of the variance.

Property. In rectangular axes, the variance of the cloud is the sum of the variances of the coordinate variables.

Target Example. The squared distances between the points of the cloud and the mean point are $(GM^1)^2 = (0 - 6)^2 + (-12 - 0)^2 = 180$, $(GM^2)^2 = 100, \ldots (GM^{10})^2 = 136$. Hence the sum of squares (from G): $(GM^1)^2 + (GM^2)^2 + \cdots + (GM^{10})^2 = 180 + 100 + \cdots + 136 = 920$, the variance of cloud $V_{cloud} = 920/10 = 92$, and the standard deviation $\sqrt{92} = 9.5917$.

One has $v_1 = 40$, $v_2 = 52$; hence $V_{cloud} = v_1 + v_2 = 92$.

Huygens' property. The variance of a cloud is equal to the mean of the squared distances from the points of the cloud to any point P, minus the squared distance between mean point G and point P:

$$V_{cloud} = \tfrac{1}{n}\sum (PM^i)^2 - (PG)^2$$

Huygens' property is the geometric extension of the following property: The variance of a variable is the mean of squares minus the squared mean.

Target Example. $\big((OM^1)^2 + (OM^2)^2 + \cdots + (OM^{10})^2\big)/10 = 128$, and $(OG)^2 = 36$. Hence $V_{cloud} = 128 - 36 = 92$.

2.3 Subclouds and Partition of a Cloud

Subclouds. *Definition*: A subset of points of a cloud is called a *subcloud*. A subcloud of a cloud is itself a cloud, with a *weight* and a mean point.

Target Example. Consider the three subclouds $\mathcal{A}$ (o) of two points $\{M^1, M^2\}$; $\mathcal{B}$ (⋆) of one point $\{M^6\}$; $\mathcal{C}$ (●) of seven points $\{M^3, M^4, M^5, M^7, M^8, M^9, M^{10}\}$.

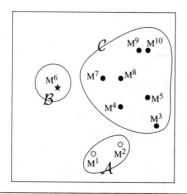 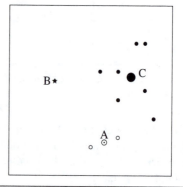

Figure 2.3 Partition of the cloud into three subclouds and the three mean points A, B, C.

The weight n_A of subcloud $\mathcal{A}$ is 2, its mean point A is the midpoint of segment M^1M^2. The weight n_B of $\mathcal{B}$ is 1, its mean point B coincides with M^6. The weight of subcloud $\mathcal{C}$ is $n_C = 7$, its mean point C is such that
$$\overrightarrow{OC} = \left(\overrightarrow{OM^3} + \ldots + \overrightarrow{OM^5} + \overrightarrow{OM^7} + \ldots + \overrightarrow{OM^{10}}\right)/7.$$
The mean points (A, B, C) of the three subclouds (Figure 2.3) can be constructed from their coordinates (Table 2.2).

Table 2.2 Coordinates of mean points A, B, and C.

	Coordinates		Weights
	x_1	x_2	
A	3	−11	$n_A = 2$
B	−8	2	$n_B = 1$
C	8.8571	2.8571	$n_C = 7$
	$\bar{x}_1 = 6$	$\bar{x}_2 = 0$	$n = 10$

The *variances* of subclouds follow. For $\mathcal{A}$, $V_{\mathcal{A}} = \left((AM^1)^2 + (AM^2)^2\right)/2 = 10$; for $\mathcal{B}$, $V_{\mathcal{B}} = 0$; for $\mathcal{C}$, $V_{\mathcal{C}} = \left((CM^3)^2 + \ldots + (CM^5)^2 + (CM^7)^2 + \ldots + (CM^{10})^2\right)/7 = 46.5306$.

Partition and between-cloud. The three subclouds $\mathcal{A}$, $\mathcal{B}$, and $\mathcal{C}$ are pairwise disjoint, and the cloud of 10 points is the union of these subclouds; therefore they constitute a *partition of the cloud* into three classes. The three mean points {A, B, C} define a new cloud called the *between-cloud* associated with the partition. The between-cloud is a *weighted cloud*, that is, each of its points is taken with the weight of the subcloud it comes from: (A,2), (B,1), (C,7). The weight of the between-cloud $(2 + 1 + 7 = 10)$ is the weight of the overall cloud. The mean point of the between-cloud is a *weighted* mean point, which coincides with G; that is, $\left(2\overrightarrow{OA} + \overrightarrow{OB} + 7\overrightarrow{OC}\right)/10 = \overrightarrow{OG}$.

> *By grouping*: Weights add up, and points "average up."

The variance of the between-cloud is the *weighted mean* of the squared distances from its points to the mean point. It is called *between-variance* and denoted by V_{between}.

Target Example. $V_{\text{between}} = \left(2\,(GA)^2 + 1\,(GB)^2 + 7\,(GC)^2\right)/10 = (260 + 200 + 114.2857)/10 = 57.4286$.

Between–within breakdown of variances. Taking point G as a reference point, let us apply Huygens' theorem to each of the subclouds $\mathcal{A}, \mathcal{B}, \mathcal{C}$; we have the three relations:

$$(GA)^2 + V_{\mathcal{A}} = \tfrac{1}{2}\left((GM^1)^2 + (GM^2)^2\right);$$
$$(GB)^2 + V_{\mathcal{B}} = (GM^6)^2;$$
$$(GC)^2 + V_{\mathcal{C}} = \tfrac{1}{7}\left((GM^3)^2 + \cdots (GM^5)^2 + (GM^7)^2 + \cdots (GM^{10})^2\right).$$

Multiplying the relations by 2, 1, and 7, respectively, then adding member by member and dividing by 10, we get:

$$\tfrac{1}{10}\left(2\,(GA)^2 + 1\,(GB)^2 + 7\,(GC)^2\right) + \tfrac{1}{10}\left(2\,V_{\mathcal{A}} + V_{\mathcal{B}} + 7\,V_{\mathcal{C}}\right)$$
$$= \tfrac{1}{10}\left((GM^1)^2 + (GM^2)^2 + \ldots + (GM^{10})^2\right),$$

that is, letting $V_{\text{within}} = (2\,V_{\mathcal{A}} + V_{\mathcal{B}} + 7\,V_{\mathcal{C}})/10$ (within-variance), we get the breakdown of variance property:

$$V_{\text{between}} + V_{\text{within}} = V_{\text{cloud}}$$

As a general definition, the *within-variance* associated with a partition will be defined as the weighted average of the variances of the subclouds of the partition.

The ratio of the between-variance to the total variance is denoted by η^2 (read "eta-square") in accordance with a classical notation (correlation ratio).

Target Example. $V_{\text{within}} = \left(2 \times 10 + 0 + 7 \times 46.5306\right)/10 = 34.5714$. Hence $V_{\text{between}} + V_{\text{within}} = 57.4286 + 34.5714 = 92 = V_{\text{cloud}}$ and $\eta^2 = (57.4286/92) = 0.624$.

2.4 Contributions

With each point of the cloud there is an amount of variance due to the point. The proportion of the variance of the cloud due to the point, denoted by Ctr, is called the *contribution of the point to the cloud.*

Target Example. The amount of variance due to point M^1 is $(1/10) \times 180 = 18$, hence the contribution $\text{Ctr}_{M^1} = 18/92 = 0.196$.

The *contribution of a subcloud* to a cloud is by definition the sum of the contributions of its points. For a subcloud, one also defines the contribution of its mean point and its within-contribution; the sum of these two contributions is the contribution of the subcloud.

Target Example. For subcloud $\mathcal{C}$, $\text{Ctr}_\mathcal{C} = \left(\frac{1}{10} \times 100 + \cdots + \frac{1}{10} \times 136\right)/92 = 0.478$. The contribution of the (weighted) mean point $(C, 7)$ is $\text{Ctr}_C = \left(\frac{7}{10}(GC)^2\right)/92 = 11.4285/92 = 0.124$; and the within-contribution is $\text{Ctr}_{\text{within}-\mathcal{C}} = \left(\frac{1}{10}(CM^3)^2 + \ldots + \frac{1}{10}(CM^5)^2 + \frac{1}{10}(CM^7)^2 + \ldots + \frac{1}{10}(CM^{10})^2\right)/92 = 0.354$.

We have $\text{Ctr}_C + \text{Ctr}_{\text{within}-\mathcal{C}} = 0.124 + 0.354 = 0.478 = \text{Ctr}_\mathcal{C}$.

If we do this for the three subclouds of the partition, we get the double *breakdown of contributions* associated with the partition.

	Contributions (Ctr) in %		
	Mean points	Within	Subclouds
$\mathcal{A}$	28.3	2.2	30.4
$\mathcal{B}$	21.7	0	21.7
$\mathcal{C}$	12.4	35.4	47.8
Total	62.4	37.6	100
	between	within	

The *between-contribution* is equal to the correlation ratio η^2, which has already been defined. The *within-contribution* is the ratio of the within-variance to the total variance and is equal to $1 - \eta^2$. For a subcloud of two points, the within-contribution amounts to the *contribution of the deviation between the two points*.

Target Example. For (A, C), define

$$\tilde{n} = \frac{1}{\frac{1}{n_A} + \frac{1}{n_C}} = \frac{1}{\frac{1}{2} + \frac{1}{7}} = \frac{14}{9} = 1.5556$$

($\tilde{n}$ may be thought of as the "weight of deviation").

Then, letting $\tilde{p} = \tilde{n}/n = 1.5556/10 = 0.15556$, one has

$$\text{Ctr}_{(AC)} = \frac{\tilde{p}\,(AC)^2}{V_{\text{cloud}}} = \frac{0.15556 \times 226.3265}{92} = 0.383.$$

Note on contributions. In practice the calculation of contributions that we have presented for a two-dimensional cloud will be mainly applied to the one-dimensional clouds associated with principal axes to provide compact summaries of these clouds.

General formulas. We now give formulas for a *weighted cloud* of points M^i with weight $n_i \geq 0$. We denote $n = \sum n_i$ the total weight (with $n > 0$) and $p_i = n_i/n$ the *relative weight* of point M^i. When all the weights are equal to 1, the cloud is said to be *elementary* (e.g., the 10-point cloud of the Target Example).

- *Mean point* or *barycenter*: $G = \sum p_i\, M^i$ and (barycentric property) $\sum p_i\, \overrightarrow{GM^i} = \overrightarrow{0}$. For equally weighted points, the barycenter is called *equibarycenter*.

- *Variance*: $V_{\text{cloud}} = \sum p_i\, (GM^i)^2$; cloud of 2 points (M, p) and (M', p'): $V_{\text{cloud}} = p\, p'(MM')^2$ (with $p + p' = 1$).

- *Contribution of point* M^i: $\text{Ctr}_i = (p_i(GM^i)^2)/V_{\text{cloud}}$. The formula extends to mean points.

- *Contribution of deviation* between the two points A and B (with weights n_A and n_B):

$$\text{Ctr}_{(AB)} = \frac{\tilde{p}\,(AB)^2}{V_{\text{cloud}}} \quad \text{with} \quad \tilde{p} = \left(\frac{1}{\frac{1}{n_A} + \frac{1}{n_B}}\right)/n.$$

Consider a partition of a cloud into subclouds. A subcloud of the cloud is denoted by C_k, its relative weight p_k, its mean point C^k, and its variance V_{C_k}.

- *Between-variance*: $V_{between} = \sum p_k (GC^k)^2$.
- *Within-variance*: $V_{within} = \sum p_k V_{C_k}$.
- *Correlation ratio*: $\eta^2 = V_{between}/V_{within}$.

2.5 Principal Axes of a Cloud

Projection of a Cloud

Let $\mathcal{L}$ and $\mathcal{L}'$ be nonparallel lines, and P be a point in the plane; the projection of point P on $\mathcal{L}$ along $\mathcal{L}'$ is the point P$'$ on $\mathcal{L}$ such that PP$'$ is parallel to $\mathcal{L}'$ (Figure 2.4). The vector $\overrightarrow{P'P}$ is called the *residual deviation*. If P is on $\mathcal{L}$, one has P$' = $ P and $\overrightarrow{P'P} = \overrightarrow{0}$.

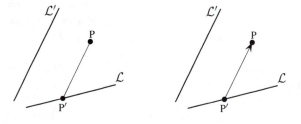

Figure 2.4 Point P$'$, projection of point P on $\mathcal{L}$ along $\mathcal{L}'$, and residual deviation (vector).

If I is the midpoint of P and Q, the projection I$'$ of I on $\mathcal{L}$ is the midpoint of P$'$ and Q$'$.

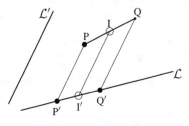

Figure 2.5 Mean point property: The midpoint is preserved by projection.

The *projected cloud* of a cloud is the cloud of its projected points, with the *mean point property*: The projection of the mean point of the cloud is the mean point of the projected cloud.

Orthogonal projection. The orthogonal projection of point P (not on $\mathcal{L}$) on $\mathcal{L}$ is the point P$'$ on $\mathcal{L}$ such that PP$'$ is perpendicular to $\mathcal{L}$ (Figure 2.6). Among all the points on $\mathcal{L}$, point P$'$ is the point at the minimal distance from point P.

Contracting property: If P$'$ and Q$'$ are the orthogonal projections of points P and Q on $\mathcal{L}$, one has P$'$Q$'$ $\leq$ PQ (with P$'$Q$'$ $=$ PQ if PQ is parallel to $\mathcal{L}$), that is, orthogonal projection contracts distances (Figure 2.6). As a consequence, the variance of an orthogonally projected cloud is always less than (or equal to) the variance of the initial cloud.

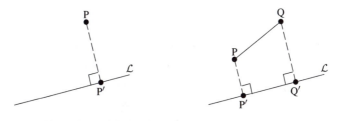

Figure 2.6 Point P$'$, orthogonal projection of point P on $\mathcal{L}$ (left), and contracting property (right).

Only orthogonal projections will be used in what follows.

Projected Clouds on Several Lines and Principal Axes

If the cloud is projected on nonparallel lines, the variances of the projected clouds differ.

Target Example. For a horizontal line, the variance of the projected cloud is $v_1 = 40$; for a vertical line, it is $v_2 = 52$ (Figure 2.7, p. 26).

In Figure 2.8 (p. 26) are represented the projected clouds on six lines whose angles with the horizontal axis are $-90°$ ($\mathcal{L}_1$), $-60°$, $-30°$, $0°$, $30°$, $60°$ ($\mathcal{L}_6$), $90°$ ($\mathcal{L}_1$). Figure 2.9 (p. 27) shows the variance of the projected cloud as a function of the angle of the line with the horizontal axis.

First principal axis. For the angle $\alpha_1 = 63.44$ degrees, the variance of the projected cloud is maximal and equal to 56; once directed (in an arbitrary way), the corresponding line is called the *first principal axis*, denoted by $\mathcal{A}_1$.

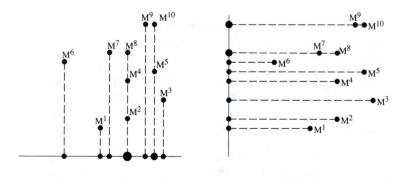

Figure 2.7 *Target Example*. Projected clouds on horizontal line ($v_1 = 40$) and on vertical line ($v_2 = 52$) with sizes of circles proportional to the number of superposed points.

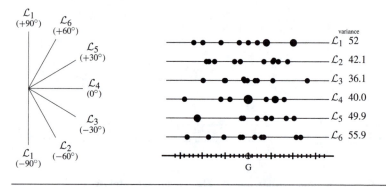

Figure 2.8 Projected clouds on six lines with their variances.

The projected cloud on $\mathcal{A}_1$ is the *first principal cloud*; its variance is also called the *variance of axis* 1, or the first *eigenvalue*, and is denoted by λ_1 (read "lambda 1").

Residual deviations. Recall (Section 2.5, p. 24) that the residual deviation of a point is the vector joining its projection to the point. Maximizing the variance of the projected cloud amounts to minimizing the sum of the squares of residual deviations; that is, the first principal cloud is the best fit of the cloud "in the sense of orthogonal least squares."

Second principal axis. If one now considers an axis $\mathcal{A}_2$ perpendicular to $\mathcal{A}_1$ going through point G, the projected cloud on $\mathcal{A}_2$ defines the second principal cloud; its variance is called second eigenvalue and denoted by λ_2, with $\lambda_2 = 36$. The sum of eigenvalues is equal to the variance of the cloud $\sum \lambda = V_{\text{cloud}}$.

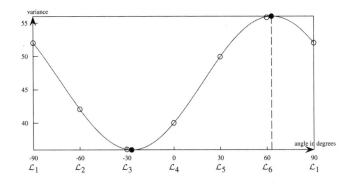

Figure 2.9 Variance of projected cloud as a function of angle.

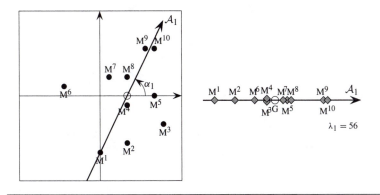

Figure 2.10 First principal axis (left) and first principal cloud (right).

Target Example: $\lambda_1 + \lambda_2 = 56 + 36 = 92$.

Principal representation of the cloud. One goes from initial axes to principal axes by a rotation through the angle $\alpha_1 = +63.44$ degrees. Equivalently, after a rotation through the angle $-\alpha_1$, one obtains the principal representation of the cloud where the first principal axis is horizontal and the second is vertical, which is the usual representation in GDA (Figure 2.12).

Quality of fit of an axis and quality of representation of a point

The *variance rate* of an axis is defined as the ratio of the variance of the axis (λ) to the variance of the (V_{cloud}). The variance rate defines the quality of fit of the axis.

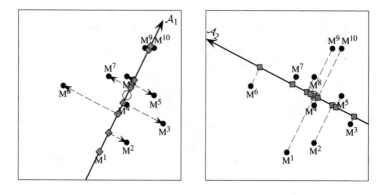

Figure 2.11 *Target Example.* First principal cloud and residual deviations (left); second principal cloud (right).

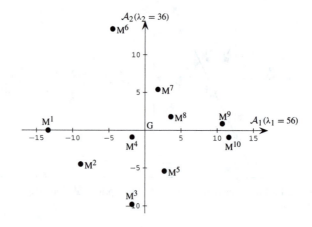

Figure 2.12 *Target Example.* Principal representation of the cloud.

Target Example. For the first principal axis, the variance rate is $\lambda_1 / V_{\text{cloud}} = 56/92 = 0.609$; the first principal axis accounts for 60.9% of the variance of the cloud. For the second one, it is $\lambda_2 / V_{\text{cloud}} = 36/92 = 0.391$.

The variance rate is a *global* index of quality of fit. For various points of the cloud, the fit qualities may differ. For instance, on axis 1, point M^1 is perfectly represented, whereas point M^6 is poorly represented (Figure 2.12). As a general definition, the *quality of representation* of a point M on an axis is the ratio of the squared distance from point M to point G along the axis to the squared distance from M to G in the space. If M' denotes the orthogonal projection of point M on an axis, the quality of representation of point M on the axis is

$$\frac{(GM')^2}{(GM)^2} = \cos^2\theta; \cos\theta = \frac{GM'}{GM}.$$

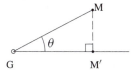

Principal coordinates and contributions of points to axes

The cloud referred to its principal axes is defined by the principal coordinates of its points (Table 2.3, p. 30). The principal coordinates define the *principal variables*. For each principal variable, it can be verified that the mean is null and the variance is equal to the eigenvalue (up to rounding errors). *The principal variables are uncorrelated*, that is, their covariance (hence their correlation) is null.

The *contribution of a point to an axis* is equal to the relative weight multiplied by the squared coordinate and divided by the eigenvalue (definition p. 22).

It is usual to present, together with the principal coordinates, the contributions and the qualities of representation of points (Table 2.3).

Note on relative contributions. Both the contribution of a point to an axis (Ctr) and the quality of representation ($\cos^2$) are relative contributions, since both are obtained by dividing the amount of variance of axis due to the point, by the variance of axis (Ctr) and by the amount of the overall variance due to the point ($\cos^2$), respectively.

Target Example. The amount of variance of axis 1 due to point M^2 is equal to $(1/10)(-8.94)^2 = 8.0$.

The variance of axis 1 is $\lambda_1 = 56$, hence the contribution $Ctr_{M^2} = 8.0/56 = 0.143$ (14.3%).

The overall amount of variance due to point M^2 is $p \times (GM^2)^2 = (1/10) \times 100 = 10$. Hence $\cos^2\theta = 8.0/10 = 0.80$ ($\theta = 26.57°$). It is why this contribution is also called the *contribution of axis to point*.

The four points (M^1, M^2, M^9, M^{10}) together contribute 91.1% to the variance of axis 1. The coordinate of the barycenter of M^1 and M^2 is

Table 2.3 *Target Example*. Principal coordinates, contributions (Ctr in %) and qualities of representation of points ($\cos^2$).

| | Coordinates | | | Ctr (in %) | | | $\cos^2$ | |
	Axis 1	Axis 2		Axis 1	Axis 2		Axis 1	Axis 2
M^1	−13.42	0.00		32.1	0		1.00	0.00
M^2	−8.94	−4.47		14.3	5.6		0.80	0.20
M^3	−1.79	−9.84		0.6	26.9		0.03	0.97
M^4	−1.79	−0.89		0.6	0.2		0.80	0.20
M^5	+2.68	−5.37		1.3	8.0		0.20	0.80
M^6	−4.47	+13.42		3.6	50.0		0.10	0.90
M^7	+1.79	+5.37		0.6	8.0		0.10	0.90
M^8	+3.58	+1.79		2.3	0.9		0.80	0.20
M^9	+10.73	+0.89		20.6	0.2		0.99	0.01
M^{10}	+11.63	−0.89		24.1	0.2		0.99	0.01
Means	0	0	Sum	100	100			
Var (λ)	56	36						

$(-13.42 - 8.94)/2 = -11.18$, and that of M^9 and M^{10} is $(+10.73 + 11.63)/2 = +11.18$. Hence the contribution of the deviation between the two barycenters (formula on p. 23, with $\tilde{n} = 1$):

$$\frac{\frac{1}{10}(11.18 + 11.18)^2}{56} = 0.893.$$

As can be seen, axis 1 is well summarized by the deviation between these two barycenters.

Similarly, axis 2 can be summarized by the deviation between M^6 and M^3; the sum of contributions of M^6 and M^3 is 77% and the contribution of the deviation is 75%.

The contributions of points to axes are used for summarizing a principal axis by its most contributing points.

2.6 From Two-Dimensional to Higher-Dimensional Clouds

Three-dimensional cloud. For a three-dimensional cloud, the extension is straightforward. The first principal axis is such that the variance of the orthogonal projection of the cloud on the axis is maximal, or equivalently the sum of squares of residual deviations is minimal. Projecting the cloud on the plane perpendicular to the first axis yields a residual two-dimensional cloud, whose principal axes are sought as has already been done for a plane cloud, and provide the second and the third principal axes of the three-dimensional cloud.

The *heredity property* (alias nesting property) states that the plane that best fits the cloud is the one determined by the first two principal axes.[2]

Higher-dimensional cloud. Thanks to multidimensional geometry, which extends the properties of elementary geometry, the approach is conceptually the same.

The mean point and the variances only depend on the distances between the points of the cloud; hence the determination of the first principal axis by orthogonal least squares, then the residual subcloud, the second principal axis, etc.

Properties

- If L denotes the dimensionality of the cloud, there are L eigenvalues $\lambda_1 \geq \lambda_2 \ldots \geq \lambda_L$; the sum of eigenvalues (variances of principal axes) is equal to the overall variance: $\sum \lambda = V_{\text{cloud}}$.

- The principal axes are pairwise orthogonal.

- Each axis can be directed arbitrarily.

- The principal variables associated with distinct eigenvalues are non-correlated.

Note on eigenvalues. Some eigenvalues may be equal. For instance, if $\lambda_1 = \lambda_2$, all the lines of the first principal plane have the same variance. If the L eigenvalues are equal, the cloud is said to be *spherical*.

The *shape of a cloud* is determined by the degree of separation of its eigenvalues. For instance, if $\lambda_1 \simeq \lambda_2 \gg \lambda_3$, that is, λ_1 and λ_2 are close to each other and markedly larger than λ_3, the cloud has the shape of a lens. If $\lambda_1 \gg \lambda_2 \simeq \lambda_3$, the cloud has the shape of a cigar.

Technically, the principal axes are determined by diagonalization or singular value decomposition (SVD) procedures, applied to matrices constructed from the data table, as will be exemplified in the case of MCA in the Appendix (p. 103).

---

[2] Such a desirable property does not hold for all multidimensional methods. For instance, it does not hold for nonmetric MDS. Similarly in regression, if one has several independent variables $(x_1, x_2, x_3, x_4 \ldots)$, the best fit of y by one variable may be provided by x_1 and the best fit by two variables may be provided by (x_2, x_4), thus x_1 is not necessarily included.

2.7 Computation Formulas
for a Weighted Cloud in a Plane

The computation formulas will enable the reader to find all numerical results from Table 2.1 (p. 17), up to a desirable accuracy.

- Distance MM′ from initial coordinates (x_1, x_2) for M and (x_1', x_2') for M′:

$$MM' = \sqrt{(x_1 - x_1')^2 + (x_2 - x_2')^2}$$

Example: $M^1 M^2 = \sqrt{(0-6)^2 + (-12+10)^2} = \sqrt{40} = 6.3$.

- Variance of x_1 (abscissas): $v_1 = \sum n_i (x_1^i - \bar{x}_1)^2 / n$.
  Variance of x_2 (ordinates): $v_2 = \sum n_i (x_2^i - \bar{x}_2)^2 / n$.
  Covariance of (x_1, x_2): $c = \sum n_i (x_1^i - \bar{x}_1)(x_2^i - \bar{x}_2) / n$.

Example: $n_i = 1$ for all M^i; $n = 10$; $v_1 = 40$, $v_2 = 52$ and $c = 8$.

- Variance of axis of angle α with horizontal axis:

$$V(\alpha) = v_1 \cos^2 \alpha + 2c \sin \alpha \cos \alpha + v_2 \sin^2 \alpha$$

Example: For $\alpha = 60°$ (line $\mathcal{L}_6$): $V(60) = 40 \times 0.25 + 2 \times 8 \times 0.866 \times 0.5 + 52 \times 0.75 = 55.9$.

- Equation for eigenvalues: $\lambda^2 - (v_1 + v_2)\lambda + v_1 v_2 - c^2 = 0$
  Variance of the first principal axis:

$$\lambda_1 = \frac{v_1 + v_2}{2} + \frac{1}{2}\sqrt{(v_1 - v_2)^2 + 4c^2}.$$

Example: $\lambda_1 = \frac{40 + 52}{2} + \frac{1}{2}\sqrt{(40 - 52)^2 + 4 \times 8^2} = 56$.

- Angle α_1 for the first principal axis: $\tan \alpha_1 = \dfrac{\lambda_1 - v_1}{c}$.

Example: $\tan \alpha_1 = (56 - 40)/8 = 2$, $\alpha_1 = 63°4$.
Equation of axis 1: $x_2 - 0 = 2(x_1 - 6)$.

- Principal coordinate y_1 of point M on the first principal axis: $y_1 = (x_1 - \bar{x}_1) \cos \alpha_1 + (x_2 - \bar{x}_2) \sin \alpha_1$.

Example: $\cos \alpha_1 = 1/\sqrt{5} = 0.4472$; $\sin \alpha_1 = 2/\sqrt{5} = 0.8944$.
Principal coordinate y_1^1 of point M^1 on axis 1:
$y_1^1 = (0 - 6) \times 0.4472 + (-12 - 0) \times 0.8944 = -13.42$.

- Distance MM′ from principal coordinates (y_1, y_2) for M and (y'_1, y'_2) for M′:

$$MM' = \sqrt{(y_1 - y'_1)^2 + (y_2 - y'_2)^2}.$$

Example: $(M^1 M^2)^2 = (-13.42 + 8.94)^2 + (0 + 4.47)^2 = 40$ (Table 2.3, p. 30); $M^1 M^2 = \sqrt{40} = 6.3$.

CHAPTER 3. THE METHOD OF MULTIPLE CORRESPONDENCE ANALYSIS

To present multiple correspondence analysis, it will be convenient to adopt the language of questionnaire.[1] The basic data set for MCA is an Individuals × Questions table. Questions are categorized variables, that is, with a finite number of *categories*, also called *modalities*. If, for each question, each individual "chooses" one and only one response category, the table is said to be in standard format. If not, a preliminary phase of *coding* is necessary. *Categories* may be qualitative (categorical or nominal), or may result from the splitting of quantitative variables into categories. *Individuals* may be persons or "statistical individuals" (firms, items, etc.).

Plan of Chapter 3. We first present the principles of MCA, starting with the distance between individuals, then we discuss the properties of the cloud of individuals and of the cloud of categories, and we proceed with principal axes, principal coordinates, contributions, and transition formulas (Section 3.1). We go on with the extensive analysis of the Taste Example (Section 3.2). Finally we present two variants of MCA (Section 3.3).

3.1 Principles of MCA

Denoting I the set of n individuals and Q the set of questions, the data table analyzed by MCA is an $I \times Q$ table, such that the entry in cell (i, q) is the category of question q chosen by individual i. The set of categories of question q is denoted by K_q and the overall set of categories is denoted by K. The number of individuals who have chosen category k is denoted by n_k (with $n_k > 0$); we denote $f_k = n_k/n$ the relative frequency of individuals who have chosen category k.

MCA yields two clouds of points: the cloud of individuals and the cloud of categories.

Overall Clouds

Cloud of individuals. In MCA, the distance between individuals is defined as follows.

---

[1] The language of questionnaire is proper in surveys with persons responding to questions; it is metaphorical when "individuals" are described by properties or attributes.

If, for question q, individuals i and i' choose the same response category ("agreement question"), the part of the distance due to question q, denoted by $d_q(i, i')$, is null: $d_q(i, i') = 0$.

The distance between two individuals is created by the questions for which they choose different categories ("disagreement questions"). Supposing that for question q, individual i chooses category k and individual i' chooses category k' different from k, the part of the squared distance between individuals i and i' due to question q is defined by the formula

$$d_q^2(i, i') = \frac{1}{f_k} + \frac{1}{f_{k'}}.$$

Denoting Q the number of questions,[2] then the overall squared distance between i and i' is defined by the formula

$$d^2(i, i') = \frac{1}{Q} \sum_{q \in Q} d_q^2(i, i').$$

The set of all distances between individuals determines the cloud of individuals consisting of n points in a space whose dimensionality is L, with $L \leq K - Q$ (overall number K of categories minus number Q of questions), and assuming $n \geq L$.

If M^i denotes the point representing individual i and G the mean point of the cloud, the squared distance from point M^i to point G is

$$(GM^i)^2 = \left(\frac{1}{Q} \sum_{k \in K_i} \frac{1}{f_k} \right) - 1,$$

where K_i denotes the *response pattern* of individual i, that is, the set of the Q categories chosen by individual i.

The *variance of the cloud* is $\sum (GM^i)^2 / n$ (see definition in Section 2.2, p. 16). It can be shown that it is equal to $(K/Q) - 1$ (average number of categories per question minus 1).

Remark. Since each individual chooses one and only one category per question, every question q with K_q categories induces a partition of the n individuals into K_q classes.

Comments

1. The smaller the frequencies of disagreement categories, the greater the distance between individuals.

---

[2] As a general rule, we denote by the same letter a finite set and its number of elements. As an exception, the number of individuals is denoted by n (rather than I).

2. If individual i chooses infrequent categories, the point M^i is far from the center; as a consequence the individuals who choose infrequent categories are located at the periphery of the cloud.

3. The variance of the cloud does not depend on data.[3]

Distance and disjunctive table. Let us denote $\delta_{ik} = 1$ if i has chosen k and if not, $\delta_{ik} = 0$, hence the disjunctive $I \times K$ table of 0 and 1. The squared distance between i and i' can be expressed by the formula:
$$d^2(i, i') = (1/Q) \sum_{k \in K} (\delta_{ik} - \delta_{i'k})^2 / f_k.$$

Example. Consider the case of three questions denoted by A, B, C, with $A = \{a1, a2\}$, $B = \{b1, b2\}$, and $C = \{c1, c2, c3\}$. Hence $K = 2 + 2 + 3 = 7$.

Table 3.1 displays the $I \times Q$ table and the disjunctive $I \times K$ table, showing an individual i with response pattern $(a1, b2, c2)$ and an individual i' with response pattern $(a2, b2, c3)$.

Table 3.1 $I \times Q$ table and disjunctive $I \times K$ table for $Q = 3$ questions and $K = 2 + 2 + 3 = 7$ categories.

| | | Q | | | | K | | | | | | |
		A	B	C		$a1$	$a2$	$b1$	$b2$	$c1$	$c2$	$c3$
i	$a1$	$b2$	$c2$		i	1	0	0	1	0	1	0	$3 = Q$
i'	$a2$	$b2$	$c3$		i'	0	1	0	1	0	0	1	$3 = Q$
	n	n	n	$3n = Qn$		n_{a1}	n_{a2}	n_{b1}	n_{b2}	n_{c1}	n_{c2}	n_{c3}	$3n = Qn$

Then we have $d^2(i, i')$

$$= \tfrac{1}{3}\left(\frac{(1-0)^2}{f_{a1}} + \frac{(0-1)^2}{f_{a2}} + \frac{(0-0)^2}{f_{b1}} + \frac{(1-1)^2}{f_{b2}} + \frac{(0-0)^2}{f_{c1}} + \frac{(1-0)^2}{f_{c2}} + \frac{(0-1)^2}{f_{c3}} \right)$$

$$= \tfrac{1}{3}\left(\frac{1}{f_{a1}} + \frac{1}{f_{a2}} + \quad 0 \quad + \quad \frac{1}{f_{c2}} + \frac{1}{f_{c3}} \right)$$

This brings us back to the distance formula given on p. 35.

Similarly, one has $(GM^i)^2 = \left(\frac{1}{Q} \sum_{k \in K} \frac{\delta_{ik}}{f_k} \right) - 1.$

---

[3] For the PCA of a correlation matrix, a similar property holds: The variance of the cloud is equal to the number of variables.

Cloud of categories. The cloud of categories is a weighted cloud of K points. Category k is represented by a point denoted by M^k with weight n_k. For each question, the sum of the weights of category points is n, hence for the whole set K the sum is nQ. The relative weight p_k of point M^k is $p_k = n_k/(nQ) = f_k/Q$; for each question, the sum of the relative weights of category points is $1/Q$, hence for the whole set the sum is 1.

$$p_k = \frac{n_k}{nQ} = \frac{f_k}{Q} \text{ with } \sum_{k \in K_q} p_k = 1/Q \text{ and } \sum_{k \in K} p_k = 1.$$

If $n_{kk'}$ denotes the number of individuals who have chosen both categories k and k', the squared *distance* between M^k and $M^{k'}$ is given by the formula

$$(M^k M^{k'})^2 = \frac{n_k + n_{k'} - 2n_{kk'}}{n_k\, n_{k'}/n}.$$

The numerator is the number of individuals who have chosen either k or k' but *not* both. For two different questions q and q', the denominator is the familiar "theoretical frequency" for the cell (k, k') of the $K_q \times K_{q'}$ two-way table.

Remark. If k and k' are two different categories of the same question, then $n_{kk'} = 0$ and $(M^k M^{k'})^2 = (1/f_k) + (1/f_{k'})$. Notice that this quantity is equal to the part of the squared distance between two individuals having chosen two different categories for the question—namely, k and k' (see p. 35).

- The *mean point* of the cloud is denoted by G (as for the cloud of individuals). *Property*: The mean point of the subcloud of categories of any question is G.

- The squared *distance* from M^k to G is

$$(GM^k)^2 = \frac{1}{f_k} - 1.$$

- By definition, the *variance of the cloud* is $\sum p_k (GM^k)^2$, that is, $(K/Q) - 1$.

The cloud of categories has the same dimensionality and the same variance as the cloud of individuals. We denote V_{cloud} the common value.

$$V_{\text{cloud}} = \frac{K}{Q} - 1$$

Comments

1. The more categories k and k' have been chosen by the same individuals, the smaller the distance $\mathrm{M}^k\mathrm{M}^{k'}$.

2. The less frequent a category k, the farther the point M^k is from the center of the cloud.

3. The cosine of the angle between $\overrightarrow{\mathrm{GM}}^k$ and $\overrightarrow{\mathrm{GM}}^{k'}$ is the tetrachoric-point correlation, that is, $\dfrac{f_{kk'}-f_k f_{k'}}{\sqrt{f_k(1-f_k)f_{k'}(1-f_{k'})}}$.

- *Contributions.* By definition, the *contribution of category point* M^k to the overall variance is the ratio of the amount of the variance of the cloud due to category k (equal to $p_k(\mathrm{GM}^k)^2$) to the overall variance. The contribution is denoted by Ctr_k with

$$\mathrm{Ctr}_k = \frac{p_k(\mathrm{GM}^k)^2}{V_{\mathrm{cloud}}} = \frac{(1-f_k)/Q}{(K-Q)/Q} = \frac{1-f_k}{K-Q}.$$

Contributions add up by grouping. The contribution of a question q is the sum of the contributions of its categories, that is $\mathrm{Ctr}_q = \frac{K_q-1}{K-Q}$. The sum of the contributions of all categories ($\sum \mathrm{Ctr}_k$) or of all questions ($\sum \mathrm{Ctr}_q$) is equal to 1.

Contribution of category k	Contribution of question q
$\mathrm{Ctr}_k = \dfrac{1-f_k}{K-Q}$	$\mathrm{Ctr}_q = \dfrac{K_q-1}{K-Q}$

Comments

1. The contribution of a category depends on data (through f_k), whereas that of a question only depends on the number of categories of the question. The more categories a question has, the more the question contributes to the variance of the cloud. This is why questions with overly disproportionate numbers of categories should be avoided. It is recommended to construct questions having about an equal number of categories, possibly after grouping. At least, it is advisable to balance various sets of questions that pertain to the same headings (see Section 6.2, p. 97). If all questions have the same number of categories $\overline{K}$, the overall variance is $\overline{K} - 1$ and the questions contribute equally to the variance ($\mathrm{Ctr}_q = 1/Q$).

2. The less frequent a category, the more it contributes to the overall variance. This property enhances infrequent categories, and this is desirable up to a certain point. Very infrequent categories of active variables (say, of frequencies less than 5%) need to be pooled with others whenever feasible; alternatively, specific MCA can be used (see Section 3.3, p. 61).

Principal clouds

Principal axes. In accordance with the geometric approach presented in Section 2, each cloud will be referred to its *principal axes* $\ell = 1, 2, \ldots L$. The principal axes are rectangular; they cross at the barycenter of the cloud; they are arbitrarily directed. The variance of the projected cloud on axis ℓ is called the *variance of axis* ℓ, or ℓth eigenvalue, denoted by λ_ℓ.

The first principal axis provides the best one-dimensional fit of the cloud (in the orthogonal least square sense), and the variance of the projected cloud on axis 1 is λ_1. Similarly, the plane generated by principal axes 1 and 2, or principal plane 1-2, provides the best two-dimensional fit, with variance $\lambda_1 + \lambda_2$, and so on.

Fundamental properties

1. The two clouds have the same variances (eigenvalues) axis by axis; for any ℓ, one has $\lambda_\ell \leq 1$.

2. The sum of eigenvalues is the variance of the whole cloud (see Section 2.6, p. 30): $\sum \lambda_\ell = V_{\text{cloud}} = \frac{K}{Q} - 1$.

Variance rates and modified rates. The *variance rate* of axis ℓ is

$$\tau_\ell = \frac{\lambda_\ell}{V_{\text{cloud}}} = \frac{\lambda_\ell}{\frac{K}{Q} - 1}.$$

The mean of eigenvalues is $\bar{\lambda} = (\frac{K}{Q} - 1)/(K - Q) = 1/Q$.

Owing to the high dimensionality of clouds, the variance rates of the first principal axes are usually quite low. To better appreciate the importance of the first axes, Benzécri (1992, p. 412) proposed to use *modified rates*.

For $\ell = 1, 2, \ldots \ell_{\max}$ such that $\lambda_\ell > \bar{\lambda}$, calculate

(1) the pseudo-cigenvalue $\lambda'_\ell = \left(\frac{Q}{Q-1}\right)^2 (\lambda_\ell - \bar{\lambda})^2$;

(2) the sum $S = \sum_{\ell=1}^{\ell_{\max}} \lambda'_\ell$;

then, for $\ell \leq \ell_{\max}$, the modified rates are equal to $\tau'_\ell = \lambda'_\ell / S$.

Modified rates can be interpreted as an index of the departure of the cloud from sphericity (i.e., all eigenvalues are equal).

Principal coordinates and principal variables. The principal coordinate of *individual point* M^i relative to principal axis ℓ is denoted by y^i_ℓ. The family of the I coordinates of individual points defines the numerical variable called the ℓth *principal variable on I*. The coordinate of *category point* M^k relative to principal axis ℓ is denoted by y^k_ℓ. The family of the K coordinates of category points defines the numerical variable called the ℓth *principal variable on K*. Each principal variable is centered, and its variance is equal to the eigenvalue:

$$\sum \tfrac{1}{n} y^i_\ell = 0, \sum \tfrac{1}{n} (y^i_\ell)^2 = \lambda_\ell \text{ and } \sum p_k y^k_\ell = 0, \sum p_k (y^k_\ell)^2 = \lambda_\ell$$

Properties

1. For each question, the mean point of the category points is the mean point G of the cloud, hence the principal variables on K are centered question by question. As a consequence, the projections on an axis of the category points of a same question are located on both sides of the barycenter G. In particular, for a question with two categories, the two category points are aligned with point G.

2. The variance of question q on axis ℓ, denoted by $v_{q\ell}$, is defined by the variance of the K_q principal ℓth coordinates of the category points of question q. Hence the property: The simple mean of the variances of questions on axis ℓ is the variance of axis ℓ.

$$v_{q\ell} = \sum_{k \in K_q} \frac{n_k}{n} (y^k_\ell)^2 \quad \text{and} \quad \frac{1}{Q} \sum_q v_{q\ell} = \lambda_\ell.$$

Contributions. The *contribution of a point to an axis* is the proportion of variance of the axis due to point. If p denotes the relative weight of a point, and y its coordinate relative to the axis of variance λ, the contribution of point to axis is equal to $(p\,y^2)/\lambda$. This formula applies both to individual and category points. The contribution of individual point M^i is $\text{Ctr}_i = \left(\tfrac{1}{n}(y^i)^2\right)/\lambda$; it is an increasing function of the distance from M^i to G along the axis, therefore it does not give any further information. The contribution of category point M^k is $\text{Ctr}_k = \left(\tfrac{f_k}{Q}(y^k)^2\right)/\lambda$; it depends both on the distance from M^k to G along the axis and on the weight of the point.

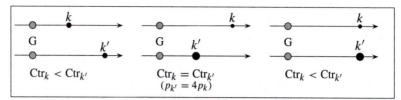

The contributions of categories to axes
constitute the main *aid to interpretation*.

The *quality of representation* of point M^k on axis ℓ is defined by (see Section 2, p. 29)

$$\cos^2 \theta_{k\ell} = \frac{(y_\ell^k)^2}{(GM^k)^2} = \frac{(y_\ell^k)^2}{\frac{1}{f_k} - 1}.$$

Property. $\cos \theta_{k\ell} = y_\ell^k / \sqrt{(1/f_k) - 1}$ is equal to the correlation of the indicator variable of k with the ℓth principal variable on I.

Transition formulas in MCA

1. For each principal axis, the coordinate y^i of individual point M^i is the simple mean of the coordinates y^k of the Q category points of the response pattern K_i of individual i, divided by $\sqrt{\lambda}$:

$$y^i = \frac{1}{\sqrt{\lambda}} \sum_{k \in K_i} y^k / Q \quad \text{(first transition formula)}.$$

2. For each principal axis, the coordinate y^k of category point M^k is the simple mean of the coordinates y^i of the n_k points of individuals $(i \in I_k)$ who have chosen category k, divided by $\sqrt{\lambda}$:

$$y^k = \frac{1}{\sqrt{\lambda}} \sum_{i \in I_k} y^i / n_k \quad \text{(second transition formula)}.$$

Remark. For each axis, the signs of the coordinates of individual points and those of category points can be chosen arbitrarily, but not independently: The transition formulas imply that, for each axis, the sign of the coordinates of individual points determines the sign of the coordinates of category points relative to the axis (and vice versa).

With the first transition formula, one goes from the cloud of categories to the cloud of individuals. With the second transition formula, one goes from the cloud of individuals to the cloud of categories.

Geometric interpretation. The individual point M^i is located at the equibarycenter[4] of the Q category points chosen by individual i, up to a stretching along the principal axes. Similarly, the category point M^k is located at the equibarycenter of the n_k points of individuals who have chosen category k, up to a stretching along the principal axes. The transition formulas will be geometrically illustrated on the Taste Example (pp. 47–50).

Matrix formulas. The matrix expressions of the transition formulas are given in the Appendix (p. 104).

Supplementary elements. The individuals and questions on which the construction of the clouds are based are called *active*. (1) A *supplementary individual* is an individual who does not participate to the construction of axes. (2) A *supplementary category* (sometimes called "illustrative category") is a category that is not used to define the distance between individuals.

The first transition formula enables one to calculate the principal coordinates of a supplementary individual whose responses to active questions are known, and to locate this individual in the cloud of individuals. The second transition formula enables one to calculate the principal coordinates of any category pertaining to a group of active individuals, and to locate this category in the cloud of categories.

Category mean points. Consider a category and the subcloud of the individuals who have chosen this category. The mean point of this subcloud of individuals is called the *category mean point*. For category k, it is denoted by $\overline{M}^k$. The ℓth principal coordinate of $\overline{M}^k$ is denoted by $\overline{y}_\ell^k$, with

$$\overline{y}_\ell^k = \sum_{i \in I_k} y^i / n_k = \sqrt{\lambda_\ell}\, y_\ell^k$$

(second transition formula, p. 41).

Each question q induces a partition of the individuals into K_q classes, so a partition of the cloud of individuals into K_q subclouds. The mean points of the K_q subclouds define the between-q cloud (see Section 2.3, p. 20). For question q, the mean point of the between-q cloud is the mean point G of the overall cloud.

---

[4] Recall (see p. 23) that equibarycenter means barycenter of *equally weighted* points.

Equivalence Properties

- The MCA of the $I \times Q$ table is equivalent to the CA of the disjunctive $I \times K$ table.

- The principal axes of MCA are those of the biweighted PCA of the K indicator variables, with weight 1 for each individual and Qf_k for the indicator variable of k (see Le Roux & Rouanet, 2004, p. 189).

- *Questionnaire with two questions A and B*: The results of the CA of the $A \times B$ contingency table can be obtained from the MCA of the $I \times Q$ table. If, in the CA of the $A \times B$ table, λ'_ℓ denotes the ℓth eigenvalue (with $\ell \leq \min(A, B) - 1$) and y'^a_ℓ the ℓth principal coordinate of point M^a, the following relations hold:

$$\lambda'_\ell = 4(\lambda_\ell - \tfrac{1}{2})^2 = (2\lambda_\ell - 1)^2; \; y'^a_\ell = \tfrac{2\lambda_\ell - 1}{\sqrt{\lambda_\ell}} \, y^a = \tfrac{2\lambda_\ell - 1}{\lambda_\ell} \, \overline{y}^a;$$

and similarly for the principal coordinates of point M^b.

The *variance rates* of the CA of the $A \times B$ table are equal to the modified rates of the MCA of the $I \times Q$ table.

- *All questions are dichotomous*: One can encode the categories of each question by $(0,1)$ and proceed with the standard PCA (PCA of correlations) of the $I \times Q$ table of 0 and 1. The eigenvalues are equal to Q times the eigenvalues of the MCA of the $I \times Q$ table, and the coordinates of individuals in PCA are equal to $\sqrt{Q}$ times those of individuals in MCA.

Burt table. Let us consider the crossing two by two of the Q questions, including the crossing of each question with itself. The symmetric $K \times K$ table obtained by juxtaposing the $Q(Q-1)$ contingency tables (each reproduced twice) and the Q diagonal tables of the category frequencies is called the Burt table (see Table 3.2, p. 44, for $Q = 3$).

Properties

1. The Φ^2 ("Phi-square") of the Burt table, denoted by Φ^2_{Burt}, is the simple mean, denoted by $\overline{\Phi}^2$, of the Φ^2 of the $Q(Q-1)/2$ contingency tables.[5]

$$\Phi^2_{\text{Burt}} = \tfrac{1}{Q}(\tfrac{K}{Q} - 1) + \tfrac{Q-1}{Q}\overline{\Phi}^2.$$

---

[5] Recall that, by definition, the Φ^2 (classical mean square contingency coefficient) of a two-way table is equal to

$$\frac{1}{n} \sum \frac{(n_{kk'} - \frac{n_k n_{k'}}{n})^2}{\frac{n_k n_{k'}}{n}}$$

by summing over all the cells (k, k') of the table.

Table 3.2 Burt table for $Q = 3$ questions and $K = 2 + 2 + 3 = 7$ categories.

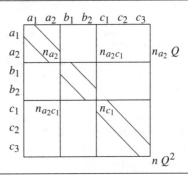

2. The CA of the Burt table produces L axes associated with L eigenvalues that are the squares of the eigenvalues of the MCA of the $I \times Q$ table. As a consequence, the Burt eigenvalues are more separate than those of the $I \times Q$ table: For each ℓ, one has:

$$\frac{\lambda_\ell^2}{\lambda_{\ell+1}^2} \geq \frac{\lambda_\ell}{\lambda_{\ell+1}} \quad \text{and} \quad \frac{\lambda_\ell^2 - \lambda_{\ell+1}^2}{\lambda_\ell^2} \geq \frac{\lambda_\ell - \lambda_{\ell+1}}{\lambda_\ell}.$$

3. For the ℓ axes such that $\lambda_\ell > \Phi_{\text{Burt}}^2 / V_{\text{cloud}} = \sum \lambda_\ell^2 / (\sum \lambda_\ell)$, the variance rates $\lambda_\ell^2 / \sum \lambda_\ell^2$ of the CA of the Burt table are greater than the variance rates $\lambda_\ell / \sum \lambda_\ell = \tau_\ell$ of the MCA of the $I \times Q$ table.

4. The CA of the Burt table produces a single cloud of category points. The ℓth principal coordinate from the Burt table associated with category k is the ℓth principal coordinate $\overline{y}_\ell^k$ of the category mean point $\overline{\text{M}}^k$ (defined on p. 42). Therefore the Burt cloud coincides with the union of the Q between-q clouds, that is, the cloud of the K category mean points.

5. The contribution of $\overline{\text{M}}^k$ to axis ℓ in the Burt cloud is equal to $p_k(\overline{y}^k)^2 / \lambda_\ell^2$; therefore it is equal to $\text{Ctr}_k = p_k(y^k)^2 / \lambda_\ell$, the contribution of M^k in the cloud of categories. As a consequence, one may proceed to the interpretation of axes from the CA of the Burt table.

Remark. The Burt table can be obtained from the Individuals $\times$ Questions table, not the reverse! The CA of the Burt table does not produce a cloud of individuals. To reinsert individuals into the analysis, one must put them as supplementary elements under their disjunctive encodings; then, as supplementary elements in the CA of the Burt table, the principal coordinates of the individuals are those from the MCA of the $I \times Q$ table.

Table 3.3 *Taste Example*. Four active questions, response frequencies (absolute n_k and relative f_k in %), and contributions (Ctr_k in %) of the 29 active categories. In bold: keywords for subsequent tables and figures.

Which, if any, of these different types of . . . television programs do you like the most	n_k	f_k in %	Ctr_k in %
News/Current affairs	220	18.1	3.3
Comedy/sitcoms	152	12.5	3.5
Police/detective	82	6.7	3.7
Nature/History documentaries	159	13.1	3.5
Sport	136	11.2	3.6
Film	117	9.6	3.6
Drama	134	11.0	3.6
Soap operas	215	17.7	3.3
Total	1215	100.0	28.0

(cinema or television) films do you like the most?			
Action/Adventure/Thriller	389	32.0	2.7
Comedy	235	19.3	3.2
Costume Drama/Literary adaptation	140	11.5	3.5
Documentary	100	8.2	3.7
Horror	62	5.1	3.8
Musical	87	7.2	3.7
Romance	101	8.3	3.7
SciFi	101	8.3	3.7
Total	1215	100.0	28.0

art do you like the most?			
Performance Art	105	8.6	3.7
Landscape	632	52.0	1.9
Renaissance Art	55	4.5	3.8
Still Life	71	5.8	3.8
Portrait	117	9.6	3.6
Modern Art	110	9.1	3.6
Impressionism	125	10.3	3.6
Total	1215	100.0	24.0

place to eat out would you like the best?			
Fish & Chips/eat-in restaurant/cafe/teashop	107	8.8	3.6
Pub/Wine bar/Hotel	281	23.1	3.1
Chinese/Thai/**Indian Rest**aurant	402	33.1	2.7
Italian Restaurant/pizza house	228	18.8	3.2
French Restaurant	99	8.1	3.7
Traditional **Steakhouse**	98	8.1	3.7
Total	1215	100.0	20.0

3.2 MCA of the Taste Example

The data involve $Q = 4$ *active variables* with $K = 8 + 8 + 7 + 6 = 29$ categories and $n = 1215$ *individuals* (those who answered the four questions).[6] The Taste Example aims at giving a fair idea of how a large data set[7] can be analyzed using MCA (see Le Roux et al., 2008).

Elementary Statistical Results

Table 3.3 (p. 45) shows the four active questions with response frequencies and contributions of categories to the overall cloud.

Among the $8 \times 8 \times 7 \times 6 = 2688$ possible response patterns, 658 are observed; the most frequent one appears 12 times. These results, compared to the number of individuals, point to a good diversity of individual responses.

Basic Results of the MCA

Variances of clouds and of axes. The *overall variance* of the clouds is equal to $(29/4)/4 - 1 = 6.25$ (formula on p. 35). The *contributions of questions* to the overall variance depend on the number of categories, that is, $(8 - 1)/(29 - 4) = 28\%, 28\%, 24\%$, and 20% (formula on p. 38). They are of the same order of magnitude.

The dimensionality of each cloud is at most $K - Q = 25$. The overall variance is the sum of eigenvalues (variances of axes); therefore the average of eigenvalues is $\bar{\lambda} = 1/Q = 0.25$. There are 12 eigenvalues exceeding the average (Table 3.4). Hereafter, we interpret the first three axes; for a justification, see Section 3.2 (p. 46).

Table 3.4 *Taste Example.* Variances of axes (eigenvalues λ_ℓ), variance rates, and modified rates.

Axes ℓ	1	2	3	4	5	6	7	8	9	10	11	12
Variances (λ_ℓ)	.400	.351	.325	.308	.299	.288	.278	.274	.268	.260	.258	.251
Variance rates	.064	.056	.052	.049	.048	.046	.045	.044	.043	.042	0.41	.040
Modified rates	.476	.215	.118	.071	.050	.030	.017	.012	.007	.002	.001	.000

---

[6] The data set can be found on the Web site of the first author.

[7] The data source is the ESRC project "Cultural Capital and Social Exclusion: A Critical Investigation." The data were collected in 2003–2004. The research team (Open University and Manchester University, UK) comprised T. Bennett, M. Savage, E. Silva, A. Warde, D. Wright, and M. Gayo-Cal.

Principal coordinates and contributions. Owing to the large number of individuals, we will only present in Table 3.6 (p. 49) the results for the six individuals displayed on p. 6.

Principal clouds of categories and of individuals. The cloud of categories in plane 1-2 has already been presented in Section 1 (Figure 1.2, p. 7), together with the one of individuals (Figure 1.3, p. 8). Figures 3.1 (p. 47) and 3.2 (p. 49) show these clouds in plane 2-3. They do not present any noticeable irregularities.

Table 3.5 (p. 48) presents the results for categories.[8] The largest contribution is that of TV-Sport on axis 3 (18.6%), but it is not overly dominating since it is closely followed by Costume Drama (13.6%).

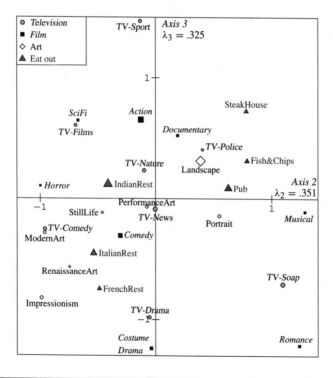

Figure 3.1 *Taste Example*. Principal cloud of the 29 categories in plane 2-3.

[8] Recall that each principal axis is arbitrarily directed, hence, the signs of coordinates on an axis can be changed *both* for categories and individuals, at the convenience of users.

Table 3.5 *Taste Example.* Active categories: relative weights $p_k = \frac{n_k}{nQ}$ (in %), principal coordinates and contributions (in %) to the first 3 axes. In bold, contributions of categories selected for the interpretation of each axis.

Television	Weights P_k	Coordinates Axis 1	Axis 2	Axis 3	Contributions (in %) Axis 1	Axis 2	Axis 3
TV-News	.0453	−0.881	−0.003	−0.087	**8.8**	0.0	0.1
TV-Comedy	.0313	+0.788	−0.960	−0.255	**4.9**	**8.2**	0.6
TV-Police	.0169	+0.192	+0.405	+0.406	0.2	0.8	0.9
TV-Nature	.0327	−0.775	−0.099	+0.234	**4.9**	0.1	0.6
TV-Sport	.0280	−0.045	−0.133	+1.469	0.0	0.1	**18.6**
TV-Film	.0241	+0.574	−0.694	+0.606	2.0	**3.3**	2.7
TV-Drama	.0276	−0.496	−0.053	−0.981	1.7	0.0	**8.2**
TV-Soap	.0442	+0.870	+1.095	−0.707	**8.4**	**15.1**	6.8
Film				Total	30.7	27.7	38.4
Action	.0800	−0.070	−0.127	+0.654	0.1	0.4	**10.5**
Comedy	.0484	+0.750	−0.306	−0.307	6.8	1.3	1.4
CostumeDrama	.0288	−1.328	−0.037	−1.240	**12.7**	0.0	**13.6**
Documentary	.0206	−1.022	+0.192	+0.522	**5.4**	0.2	1.7
Horror	.0128	+1.092	−0.998	+0.103	**3.8**	**3.6**	0.0
Musical	.0179	−0.135	+1.286	−0.109	0.1	**8.4**	0.1
Romance	.0208	+1.034	+1.240	−1.215	**5.5**	**9.1**	**9.4**
SciFi	.0208	−0.208	−0.673	+0.646	0.2	**2.7**	2.7
Art				Total	34.6	25.7	39.5
PerformanceArt	.0216	+0.088	−0.075	−0.068	0.0	0.0	0.0
Landscape	.1300	−0.231	+0.390	+0.313	1.7	**5.6**	**3.9**
RenaissanceArt	.0113	−1.038	−0.747	−0.566	**3.0**	1.8	**1.1**
StillLife	.0146	+0.573	−0.463	−0.117	1.2	0.9	0.1
Portrait	.0241	+1.020	+0.550	−0.142	**6.3**	2.1	0.1
ModernArt	.0226	+0.943	−0.961	−0.285	**5.0**	**5.9**	0.6
Impressionism	.0257	−0.559	−0.987	−0.824	2.0	**7.1**	**5.4**
Eat out				Total	19.3	23.5	11.2
Fish&Chips	.0220	+0.261	+0.788	+0.313	0.4	**3.9**	0.7
Pub	.0578	−0.283	+0.627	+0.087	1.2	**6.5**	0.1
IndianRest	.0827	+0.508	−0.412	+0.119	**5.3**	**4.0**	0.4
ItalianRest	.0469	−0.021	−0.538	−0.452	0.0	**3.9**	**2.9**
FrenchRest	.0204	−1.270	−0.488	−0.748	**8.2**	1.4	**3.5**
Steakhouse	.0202	−0.226	+0.780	+0.726	0.3	**3.5**	**3.3**
				Total	15.3	23.1	10.9

Table 3.6 *Taste Example*. Principal coordinates and contributions (in %) to the first three axes for the six individuals of Table 1.1 (p. 6).

	Coordinates			Contributions (in %)		
	Axis 1	Axis 2	Axis 3	Axis 1	Axis 2	Axis 3
1	+0.135	+0.902	+0.432	0.00	0.19	0.05
7	−0.266	−0.064	−0.438	0.01	0.00	0.05
31	+1.258	+1.549	−0.768	0.33	0.56	0.15
235	−1.785	−0.538	−1.158	0.65	0.07	0.34
679	+1.316	−1.405	−0.140	0.36	0.46	0.00
1215	−0.241	+1.037	+0.374	0.01	0.25	0.04

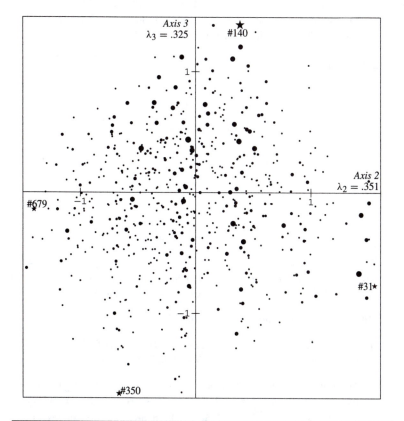

Figure 3.2 *Taste Example*. Principal cloud of individuals in plane 2-3 with typical patterns.

We will now detail the relation between the two clouds.

- *From the cloud of categories to the cloud of individuals.*

Applying the first transition formula (p. 41), the location of any individual can be reconstituted from the cloud of categories. For instance, the location of individual #235 with response pattern (TV-News, CostumeDrama, RenaissanceArt, FrenchRest) is constructed as follows:

1. In the cloud of categories, construct the *equibarycenter* (represented by a gray star in Figure 3.3, left) of the four points representing the four categories chosen by the individual.

2. *Stretch* the equibarycenter along axis 1 by the ratio $1/\lambda_1$ and along axis 2 by the ratio $1/\lambda_2$, hence the point represented by a black star in Figure 3.3 (right), which is the individual #235 represented in Figure 1.3 (p. 8). Similarly for individual #31.

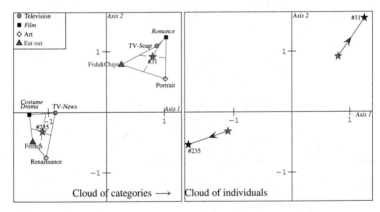

Figure 3.3 *Taste Example.* Plane 1-2: Reconstitution of individual points from their response patterns (individuals#235,#31) (halfsize).

In terms of coordinates (Table 3.5, p. 48):

1. For axis 1, we have $(-0.881-1.328-1.038-1.270)/4 = -1.12925$; and for axis 2, $(-0.003 - 0.037 - 0.747 - 0.488)/4 = -0.31875$;

2. dividing the coordinate on axis 1 by $\sqrt{\lambda_1}$ and the one on axis 2 by $\sqrt{\lambda_2}$, we have $y_1^i = -1.12925/\sqrt{0.4004} = -1.785$ and $y_2^i = -0.31875/\sqrt{0.3512} = -0.538$, which are the coordinates of the individual point #235 (Table 3.6, p. 49).

• *From the cloud of individuals to the cloud of categories.*

Applying the second transition formula (p. 41), the location of a category can be reconstituted from the cloud of individuals.

For instance, consider the category French Restaurant, which has been chosen by 99 individuals. The subcloud of these 99 individuals (◇) has a mean point represented by a gray star in Figure 3.4 (left, p. 51). Stretching this mean point along axis 1 by $1/\sqrt{\lambda_1}$ and along axis 2 by $1/\sqrt{\lambda_2}$ yields the point represented by a black star in Figure 3.4 (right); this point represents the category French Restaurant (Figure 1.2, p. 7).

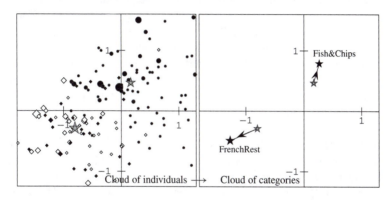

Figure 3.4 *Taste Example.* Subclouds of "French Restaurant" individuals (◇) and "Fish & Chips" individuals (•) (right) with their mean points (gray star) and reconstitution of category points (black star) (half size).

The coordinates of the mean point of the subcloud are found to be $(-0.8038, -0.2893)$, hence $-0.8038/\sqrt{0.4004} = -1.270$ and $-0.2893/\sqrt{0.3512} = -0.488$, which are the coordinates of the French Restaurant category point (Table 3.5, p. 48).

Similarly, for Fish & Chips (chosen by 107 individuals), the coordinates of the mean point of the subcloud are $(0.1651, 0.4670)$, hence the ones of the Fish & Chips point.

Interpretation of the analysis

How many axes need to be interpreted? The choice of the number of axes to be interpreted is based on the decrease of eigenvalues, the cumulated modified rates, and last but not least, the interpretability of axes.

The first eigenvalue is well separated from the second one; the difference between λ_1 and λ_2 is 12% of λ_1 ($\frac{\lambda_1-\lambda_2}{\lambda_1} = .12$), while the one between

λ_2 and λ_3 is 7% of λ_2. After axis 4, eigenvalues decrease regularly and the differences are small. Moreover, the modified rate of axis 1 is equal to .48; adding axis 2 brings the cumulated rate to .69, further adding axis 3, to .81. This is why we will interpret the first three axes.

To begin with, we notice that questions *Film* and *TV* contribute the most to the variance of axis 1 (Table 3.5, p. 48). The four questions contribute about equally to the variance of axis 2. For axis 3, *Film* and *TV* are predominant.

Guide for interpreting an axis. For the interpretation of an axis, we select all the categories whose contributions to axis exceed the average contribution (here $100/29 = 3.4\%$, baseline criterion).

For each question, we also evaluate the contribution of the deviation between the barycenter of the selected categories located on one side of the axis and the barycenter of those located on the other side, and express this contribution as a proportion of the contribution of the question (for an example of calculation, see Table 3.10, p. 57).

Interpreting axis 1. The 13 categories that meet the criterion ($\text{Ctr}_k \geq 3.4\%$), are located on each side of axis 1 for all questions, except for *Art*. This is why we add the Renaissance category with a contribution (3%) near the criterion. Except for the question *Art*, the contributions of deviations to questions are fairly good; the proportions are $26.8/30.7 = 87\%$ for *TV*, 96% for *Film*, and 84% for *Eat out* (Table 3.7).

The 14 categories together contribute 89% to the variance of axis 1; they summarize fairly well the oppositions on axis 1, which leads to the following interpretation (Figure 3.5)[9]:

- On the left, one finds Drama and Documentary films, News and Nature TV programs, and Renaissance Art, together with French Restaurant.

- On the right, one finds Romance, Comedy, and Horror Films, Soap and Comedy TV programs, and Portrait and Modern Art, together with Indian Restaurant.

***To sum up*, axis 1 opposes *matter-of-fact* (and traditional) tastes to *fiction world* (and modern) tastes.**

---

[9] When comparing Figure 3.5 with the corresponding Figure 1.2 (p. 7), the reader will appreciate the gain in readability. Just think of the full-scale analysis with 41 questions and 166 categories (Le Roux et al., 2008).

Table 3.7 *Taste Example.* Interpretation of axis 1: 14 categories with their contributions (in %), written in column "left" or "right" in accordance with Figure 3.5, and contributions of deviations per question.

● *TV* (30.7%)				■ *Film* (34.6%)			
	left	right	*deviation*		left	right	*deviation*
TV-News	8.8			CostumeDrama	12.7		
TV-Soap		8.4	*26.8*	Comedy		6.8	
TV-Nature	4.9			Romance		5.5	*33.1*
TV-Comedy	4.9			Documentary	5.4		
♦ *Art* (19.3%)				Horror		3.8	
Portrait	6.3			▲ *Eat out* (15.4%)			
Modern		5.0	*14.7*	FrenchRest	8.2		
Renaissance	3.0			IndianRest		5.3	*12.9*

Total contribution: 43.0 (left) + 46.0 (right) = 89.0

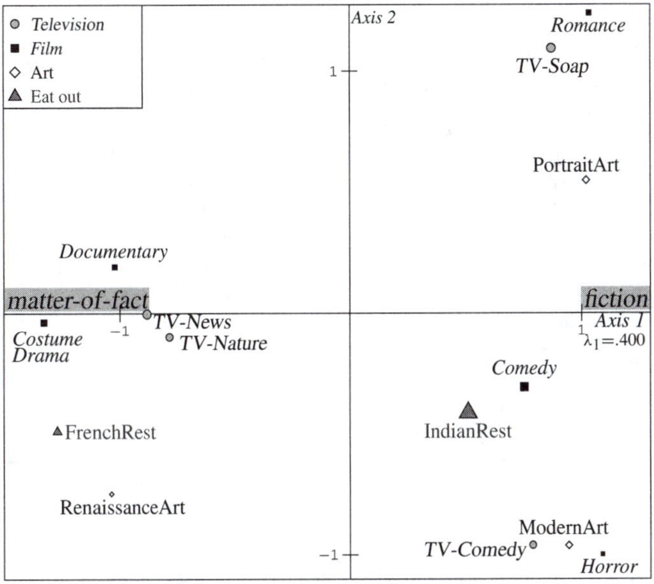

Figure 3.5 *Taste Example.* The 14 categories selected for the interpretation of axis 1 in plane 1-2.

Interpretation of axis 2. To the 13 categories meeting the criterion (3.4%), we add TV-Film with a contribution (3.3%) near the criterion. Except for *Film*, the contributions of deviations to questions are fairly good; the proportions are $26.3/27.7 = 95\%$ (*TV*), 80% (*Art*), 92% (*Eat out*), and 54% (*Film*). Adding the category "SciFi" to the question *Film* brings the contibution up to 21.7%, that is, 84% of the questions (Table 3.8). These 15 categories together contribute 91% to the variance of axis 2.

- At the top in Figure 3.6, one finds Romance and Musical films, TV-Soap, together with Landscape, and also Pub, Steak House, and Fish & Chips.

- At the bottom, one finds Horror and SciFi Films, Comedy and Film TV programs, together with Impressionism and Modern Art, and also Indian and Italian Restaurants.

To sum up, axis 2 opposes *popular* to *sophisticated* tastes.

Table 3.8 *Taste Example*. Interpretation of axis 2: 15 categories with their contributions (in %), written in columns "top" or "bottom" in accordance with Figure 3.6, and contributions of deviations per question.

	top	bottom	*deviation*		top	bottom	*deviation*
● *TV* (30.7%)				♦ *Art* (23.5%)			
TV-Soap	15.1			Impressionism		7.1	
TV-Comedy		8.2	*26.3*	Modern		5.9	*18.7*
TV-Film		3.3		Landscape	5.6		
■ *Film* (25.7%)				▲ *Eat out* (23.1%)			
Romance	9.1			Pub	6.5		
Musical	8.4		*21.7*	IndianRest		4.0	
Horror		3.6		ItalianRest		3.9	*21.3*
SciFi		2.7		Fish&Chips	3.9		
				SteakHouse	3.5		

Total: 52.1 (top) +38.7 (bottom) =90.8

Remark on contributions. Modern and Landscape category points have rather close contributions to axis 2; the first one is more distant from the center along axis 2 but with a smaller weight, whereas the second one is less distant but more weighted.

Interpretation of axis 3. Questions *TV* and *Film* together contribute 78% to the variance of axis 3, and they prevail in the interpretation of axis 3. To the 9 categories meeting the criterion (3.4%) we add Steak House

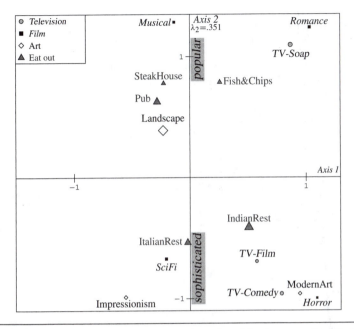

Figure 3.6 *Taste Example.* The 15 categories selected for interpretation of axis 2 in plane 1-2.

and Italian Restaurant. The contributions of deviations are all fairly good: 84% for *TV*, 85% for *Film*, 76% for *Art*, and 71% for *Eat out* (Table 3.9). These 11 categories together contribute 86% to the variance of axis 3, and summarize well the oppositions on axis 3.

Table 3.9 *Taste Example.* Interpretation of axis 3: 11 categories with their contributions (in %), written in column "top" or "bottom" in accordance with Figure 3.7, and contributions of deviations per question.

	top	bottom	*deviation*			top	bottom	*deviation*
● *TV* (38.4%)					■ *Film* (39.5%)			
TV-Sport	18.6				CostumeDrama		13.6	
TV-Drama		8.2	*32.2*		Action	10.5		*33.4*
TV-Soap		6.8			Romance		9.4	
♦ *Art* (11.2%)					▲ *Eat out* (10.9%)			
Impressionism		5.4			FrenchRest		3.5	
Landscape	3.9		*8.5*		SteakHouse	3.3		*7.7*
					ItalianRest		2.9	

Total: 36.3 (top) + 49.9 (bottom) =86.2

- At the top of Figure 3.7, one finds Action Film, Sport TV program, together with Landscape and Steak House;

- At the bottom, one finds Costume Drama and Romance films, Drama and Soap TV programs, together with Impressionism Art, and French and Italian Restaurants.

To sum up, axis 3 opposes *hard* to *soft* tastes.

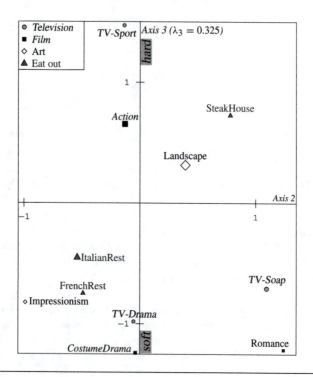

Figure 3.7   *Taste Example.* The 11 categories selected for the interpretation of axis 3 in plane 2-3.

Remark on contributions. In plane 1-2, TV-Sport point is close to the center of the cloud (Figure 1.2, p. 7), whereas on axis 3, this category point is very far from the center with a strong contribution.

This example illustrates how reckless it would be to confine the interpretation to axes 1 and 2.

Table 3.10 Contribution of the deviation between the two barycenters News&Nature and Comedy&Soap and proportion of deviation to question *TV.*

Categories		News	Nature	Comedy	Soap
	Frequency	220	159	152	215
	Coordinates	−0.881	−0.775	+0.788	+0.870

Barycenters		News&Nature	Comedy&Soap
	Frequency	$220 + 159 = 379$	$152 + 215 = 367$
	Coordinates	−0.837	+0.836

Deviation		
	Frequency	$\tilde{n}_d = 1/\left(\frac{1}{379} + \frac{1}{367}\right) = 186.452$
		$d = +0.836 - (-0.837) = 1.673$
	Ctr of deviation	$\frac{186.452}{4 \times 1215}(1.673)^2/0.4004 = 0.268$
	Proportion to question	$\frac{0.268}{0.307} = 87.2\%$

Coordinate of News&Nature: $\frac{-0.881 \times 220 \times -0.775 \times 159}{379} = -0.837$

Inspecting and "dressing up" the cloud of individuals. As already said, the cloud of individuals does not present any particular irregularities that point to a lack of homogeneity.

In plane 1-2, the cloud has a triangular shape (Figure 1.3, p. 8), whose poles will be characterized. For this purpose, one may define *typical response patterns* and construct the corresponding points as *supplementary individuals.*

Thus, for the pole "matter-of-fact," we take the four (one per question) leftmost categories (the most negative coordinates in Table 3.5, p. 48)— namely (TV-News, Costume Drama, Renaissance, French Restaurant)— and construct the corresponding point. In fact, this response pattern is the one of individual #235, already shown in Figure 1.3. Similarly, we can do so for the two other poles: For "popular-fiction" (top-left of plane 1-2), the response pattern (TV-Soap, Romance, Portrait, Fish & Chips) corresponds to individual #31; for "sophisticated-fiction" (bottom-left), the pattern (TV-Comedy, Horror, Modern, Indian Restaurant) corresponds to individual #679. For axis 3, the two opposed response patterns (TV-Drama, CostumeDrama, Impressionism, French Restaurant) (soft) and (TV-Sport, Action, Landscape, Steak House) (hard) correspond to individuals #350 and #140 (Figure 3.2, p. 49).

Constructing typical individuals is just one way to enrich the interpretation of the cloud of individuals. We may also construct *landmark*

58

individuals corresponding to various real or fabricated response patterns. For instance, let us imagine that Oscar Wilde answered the questionnaire and gave the answers (TV-Soap, Horror, Renaissance, Pub). This yields the point whose principal coordinates are found to be (0.254, −0.010, −0.475) (no corresponding observed response pattern!).[10]

In the same vein, in the cloud of individuals, various subclouds of interest may be examined to enhance the interpretation. In Section 1, we have already presented such an example (see Figure 1.4, p. 9; see also Figure 3.10, p. 61). An in-depth study of the cloud of individuals will be pursued in sections 4 and 5.

Supplementary Groups of Individuals

In addition to the basic sample, the questionnaire covered several groups of immigrants. The method of supplementary individuals makes it possible to geometrically situate the individuals of these groups with respect to the basic cloud. As an example, Figure 3.8 shows the group of 38 Indian immigrants who have answered the four questions. Most individual points of this group are located in the lower right quadrant. The coordinates of the mean point of the subcloud are (+0.316, −0.343, −0.090).

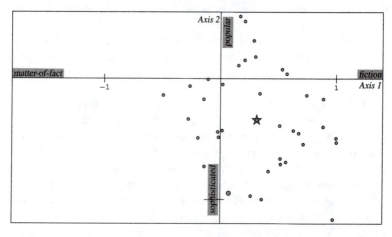

Figure 3.8 *Taste Example.* Plane 1-2. Cloud of 38 Indian immigrants with its meanpoint (★).

---

[10] Using this method, the reader may situate himself or herself. To do so, use the "locate_yourself" program on the Web site of the first author.

Supplementary Variables

In the questionnaire, status variables such as *Gender*, *Age*, and annual *Household Income* were recorded. Age was coded into six categories, and Income into six categories (from < *$9 000* to > *$60 000*) plus "unknown" category.

These variables may be introduced as supplementary variables, and their categories located in the cloud of categories. Table 3.11 shows the frequencies and coordinates on the first three axes of supplementary categories.

Table 3.11 *Taste Example.* Supplementary questions: coordinates on the first three axes for Gender, Age (six categories), and Household Income (six + "unknown" categories)

	Age					Income			
	Weight	Axis 1	Axis 2	Axis 3			Weight	Axis 1	Axis 2	Axis 3
Men	513	−0.178	−0.266	+0.526		<$9 000	231	+0.190	+0.272	+0.075
Women	702	+0.130	+0.195	−0.384		$10–19 000	251	−0.020	+0.157	−0.004
						$20–29 000	200	−0.038	−0.076	+0.003
18–24	93	+0.931	−0.561	+0.025		$30–39 000	122	−0.007	−0.071	−0.128
25–34	248	+0.430	−0.322	−0.025		$40–59 000	127	+0.017	−0.363	+0.070
35–44	258	+0.141	−0.090	+0.092		>$60 000	122	−0.142	−0.395	−0.018
45–54	191	−0.085	−0.118	−0.082		"unknown"	162	−0.092	+0.097	−0.050
55–64	183	−0.580	+0.171	−0.023						
≥ 65	242	−0.443	+0.605	+0.000						

As a rule of thumb, a deviation between categories greater than 0.5 will be deemed to be "notable"; a deviation greater than 1, definitely "large."

- *Gender*. The deviations between Men and Women are 0.308 on axis 1, 0.461 on axis 2, and 0.910 on axis 3. The deviation is notable (nearly large) on axis 3.

- *Age*. The category points are ordered along axis 1 and axis 2 (Figure 3.9, p. 60). Age is correlated to these axes. On axis 1, the deviation between the 18-24 category point and the barycenter of the last two categories (>55) is $0.931 - (-183 \times 0.580 - 242 \times 0.443)/(183 + 242) = 1.437$, which is important. On axis 2, the deviation between the 18-24 and >55 category points is $0.605 + 0.561 = 1.166$, which is a very large deviation.

- *Income*. The category points are ordered on axis 2 (Figure 3.9, p. 60). Income is correlated with axis 2.

Remark. The 162 individuals whose income is unknown may be represented in the cloud of individuals (Figure 3.10, p. 61).

60

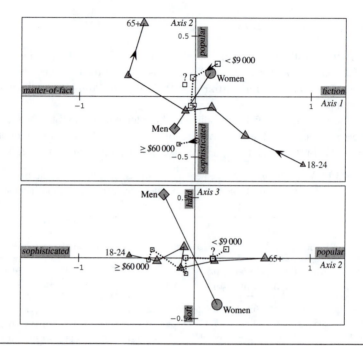

Figure 3.9 *Taste Example.* Supplementary questions in plane 1-2 (top), and in plane 2-3 (bottom) (cloud of categories).

The mean point of the subcloud is near the barycenter G of the overall cloud, and the points are rather well scattered around point G, thus discarding the conjecture of a systematic bias. This illustrates the usefulness of MCA for verifying data sets.

Thus, supplementary variables make it possible to enrich the interpretation of axes: Axis 1 is related to *Age*; axis 2 to *Income* and *Age*; axis 3 to *Gender*.

Category mean points and Burt cloud. Consider the cloud of individuals; the category mean points have been introduced on page 42 and illustrated in the case of French Restaurant and Fish & Chips (Figure 3.4, p. 51). With each question q, there are associated K_q category mean points (between-cloud of question q). If one juxtaposes on the same diagram the Q between-clouds associated with the Q questions, one gets the *cloud of the K category mean points* (Figure 3.11, p. 62), that is, the Burt cloud produced by the CA of the Burt table (see p. 44).

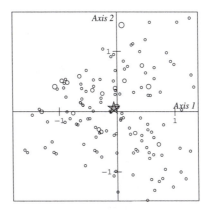

Figure 3.10 *Taste Example.* Subcloud of 162 individuals whose income is unknown with it smean point (★) in plane 1-2 (the size of this figure has been halved).

The Burt cloud is in one–one correspondence with the cloud of categories, up to shrinkings of axes (Figures 1.2, p. 7 and 3.11, p. 62) since the variances of axes are the squares of the eigenvalues. The Burt cloud, in plane 1-2, is comparatively more elongated along axis 1, since $\sqrt{\lambda_1^2/\lambda_2^2} = 1.14 > \sqrt{\lambda_1/\lambda_2} = 1.07$.

3.3 Two Variants of MCA

Two variants of MCA will be presented in this subsection (adapted from Le Roux & Rouanet, 2004, pp. 203–213):

- *Specific MCA* (SpeMCA) that consists in restricting the analysis to the categories of interest;

- *Class Specific Analysis* (CSA), which consists in analyzing a subcloud of individuals.

Specific MCA

A case in point for specific MCA is the problem of *infrequent categories* (say, <5%) of active variables. As already seen (see comments on p. 38), they participate heavily in the contribution of the variable, and they can be overly influential for the determination of axes. What should be done in the first place is to attempt to pool infrequent categories with some other

62

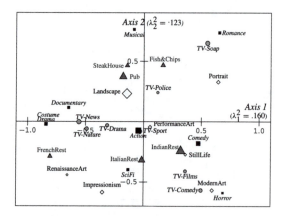

Figure 3.11 *Taste Example.* Burt cloud of the 29 category mean points in principal plane 1-2 (cloud of individuals). The scale is the same as that of the cloud of categories (Figure 1.2, p.7).

categories of the same variable. When this is not naturally feasible, it is possible, in order to preserve the constitutive properties of MCA, to resort to a variant of MCA that ignores these categories for the determination of distances between individuals.

More generally, there may be categories of active variables that one would like to discard, such as "junk" categories. By junk category, we mean a category made of heterogeneous entities, for instance "others" in a questionnaire. Such a category is properly *not representable* by a point. Finally, there is the case of missing data for some variables.

In specific MCA, these various sorts of undesirable categories may be treated as *passive categories*,[11] as opposed to active categories of active questions. Experience has shown that specific MCA permits a more refined analysis than regular MCA.

Specific cloud of individuals.   We denote d' the *specific distance* between two individuals (as opposed to d, the regular distance defined on p. 35). If, for question q, both individuals i and i' have chosen active categories, the distance is unchanged. If for a disagreement question q, individual i has chosen an active category k and individual i' a passive category k', the part of the squared distance due to q is $d'^2_q(i, i') = 1/f_k$—instead of

---

[11] "Passive categories" of active variables will be distinguished from supplementary categories, that is, categories of supplementary variables.

$(1/f_k) + (1/f_{k'})$. The overall specific distance is defined by $d'^2(i, i') = \sum d_q'^2/Q$. Specific MCA amounts to studying the orthogonal projection of the overall cloud of individuals on the subspace associated with active categories. The projected cloud is called *specific cloud*. One has $d'(i, i') \leq d(i, i')$ (contracting property).

Specific cloud of categories. It is the subcloud of the K' active categories, with the same weights $p_k = f_k/Q$ and the same distance as in regular MCA (see p. 37).

Remark. One might think of proceeding to the CA of the disjunctive table, after suppressing the columns of passive categories. However, this procedure would destroy the constitutive properties of MCA. For instance, consider a questionnaire with three questions A (2 categories), B (2 categories) and C (3 categories), individual i with response pattern $(a1, b2, c2)$, individual i' with response pattern $(a2, b2, c3)$ (Table 3.1, p. 36); suppose that category $c3$ is passive. If $c3$ is suppressed in the CA of the disjunctive table, the number of active categories chosen by i is 3, but the number of active categories chosen by i' is 2, therefore, in the CA, the numerator of the squared distance due to question B becomes $(1/3 - 1/2)^2 \neq 0$, hence the part of distance due to B—an agreement question—would not be null!

Properties

1. The common *dimensionality* of specific clouds is at most $L' = K' - Q'$, where Q' denotes the number of questions with no passive categories. The common *variance* of specific clouds is equal to

$$V_{\text{spe}} = \frac{K'}{Q} - \sum_{k \in K'} \frac{f_k}{Q},$$

with $V_{\text{spe}} \leq V_{\text{cloud}}$.

2. The eigenvalues of specific clouds will be denoted by μ_ℓ, with $\ell = 1, 2, \ldots L'$. One has $V_{\text{spe}} = \sum_{\ell=1}^{L'} \mu_\ell$.
   By analogy with regular MCA, we calculate the modified rates as follows. The mean of eigenvalues is $\overline{\mu} = V_{\text{spe}}/L'$. If $\ell_{\max}$ is such that $\mu_{\ell_{\max}} < \overline{\mu}$ and $\mu_{\ell_{\max}+1} \geq \overline{\mu}$, for $\ell = 1, \ldots \ell_{\max}$ the modified rates are equal to $(\mu_\ell - \overline{\mu})^2/S$, with $S = \sum (\mu_\ell - \overline{\mu})^2$ by summing for $\ell = 1$ to $\ell_{\max}$.

3. *Transition formulas.* Denoting $y_\ell'^i$ the coordinate of individual point M^i and $y_\ell'^k$ the coordinate of category point M^k (with relative weight $p_k = f_k/Q$) on axis ℓ, one has the two following formulas:

$$y'^i_\ell = \frac{1}{\sqrt{\mu_\ell}} \left(\sum_{k \in K'_i} y'^k_\ell / Q - \sum_{k \in K'} p_k y'^k_\ell \right) \quad \text{and} \quad y'^k_\ell = \frac{1}{\sqrt{\mu_\ell}} \sum_{i \in I_k} y'^i_\ell / n_k$$

(K'_i denotes the subset of active categories chosen by individual i). Those formulas apply to active, passive, and supplementary categories, and to active and supplementary individuals.

4. The specific principal variables on I are centered, and their variances are equal to the eigenvalues.

5. For axis ℓ, the *weighted sum* of the squared coordinates of active categories is equal to the eigenvalue: $\sum_{k \in K'} p_k (y'^k_\ell)^2 = \mu_\ell$.

Steps of specific MCA. They are the same as those of regular MCA (see p. 9), except that, for preparing the data table (Step 2), the choice of passive categories of active variables must be made. Also, for constructing the cloud of individuals, it is recommended, as a general rule, to discard the individuals who have chosen too many questions with passive categories (say, more than one fifth of the active questions).

Examples. Applications of specific MCA will be presented for full-scale research studies in Section 6 (p. 91).

Class Specific Analysis (CSA)

This variant of MCA is used to study a class (subset) of individuals with reference to the whole set of (active) individuals, that is, to determine the specific features of the class. It consists in proceeding to the search of the principal axes of the subcloud associated with the class of individuals.

- *Special notation for the present subsection.* We denote N the number of elements of I (total number of individuals), N_k the number of individuals in I who have chosen k, and $F_k = N_k/N$ the associated relative frequency. We denote I' the class of individuals, n its number of elements, n_k the number of individuals in I' who have chosen category k, and $f_k = n_k/n$ the associated relative frequency; $n_{kk'}$ the number of individuals in I' who have chosen both categories k and k'.

Class specific cloud of individuals. The distance between two individuals i and i' of the subset I' is the one defined from the whole cloud; more precisely, if for question q, i chooses k and i' chooses k', one has (using the notation of this paragraph) $d^2(i, i') = (1/F_k) + (1/F_{k'})$, while from the subquestionnaire $I' \times Q$ we would have obtained $(1/f_k) + (1/f_{k'})$.

Remark. The subcloud under study is all the more different from the one constructed by the MCA of the $I' \times Q$ subtable as the frequencies (f_k) of categories in the subset I' differ very much from the ones (F_k) in the whole set I.

Class specific cloud of categories. The distance between two categories is such that:

$$d'^2(k, k') = \frac{f_k(1 - f_k)}{F_k^2} + \frac{f_{k'}(1 - f_{k'})}{F_{k'}^2} - 2\frac{f_{kk'} - f_k f_{k'}}{F_k F_{k'}}.$$

The distance of category point M^k from the mean point of the (specific) cloud is equal to $f_k(1 - f_k)/F_k^2$. The specific subcloud of categories is weighted, and the weight of category point M^k is $p_k = F_k/Q$ (as in the whole cloud).

Properties

1. The common *variance* V_{spe} of the specific clouds is equal to

$$V_{\text{spe}} = \frac{1}{Q} \sum_{k \in K} \frac{f_k(1 - f_k)}{F_k}.$$

The contribution of category point M^k to the specific variance is

$$\text{Ctr}_k = \frac{\frac{1}{Q}\frac{f_k(1 - f_k)}{F_k}}{V_{\text{spe}}}.$$

2. *Transition formulas*

Denoting y'^i_ℓ as the specific principal coordinate of individual point M^i on axis ℓ, y'^k_ℓ as that of category point M^k, and μ_ℓ the ℓth eigenvalue of the specific clouds, one has the following transition formulas:

$$y'^i_\ell = \frac{1}{\sqrt{\mu_\ell}}\left(\sum_{k \in K_i} \frac{y'^k_\ell}{Q} - \sum_{k \in K} \frac{f_k}{Q} y'^k_\ell \right) \text{ and } y'^k_\ell = \frac{1}{\sqrt{\mu_\ell}} \sum_{i \in I'_k} y'^i_\ell / (n F_k),$$

where I'_k denotes the subset of individuals of I' who have chosen category k.

3. The principal variables on I' are centered and their variances are equal to the specific eigenvalues (μ_ℓ).

4. The principal variables on K, weighted by $p_k = F_k/Q$, are centered and their variances are equal to the specific eigenvalues.

The *steps of CSA* are the same as those of regular MCA (see p. 9), and the interpretation of axes is performed in the same way.

Taste Example

We will briefly comment on the specific analysis of the 183 individuals of the 55-64 age group. This group comprises 99 women and 84 men. Some active categories are overrepresented: TV-News with frequency 0.30 versus 0.18 for the 1215 individuals, Costume Drama (0.23 vs. 0.12), TV-Nature (0.22 vs. 0.13), and French Restaurant (0.15 vs. 0.08).

The specific variance of the subcloud is equal to 5.745. The first specific eigenvalues are equal to 0.5913, 0.4946, 0.4351, 0.3710, 0.3495, etc. Cumulated modified rates are equal to 0.45, 0.69, 0.93, etc.

Table 3.12 gives the contributions of the four questions to specific variance and to the first two specific axes.

Note that the contributions of questions to the specific variance are of the same order of magnitude, but for the second specific axis, the contribution of *TV* is predominant (61%). Thus, we will interpret the first axis, which shows the most important cleavage inside the group, and summarize the interpretation of the second axis.

Table 3.12 Contributions of the 4 questions to the specific variance and to specific axes 1 and 2.

	TV	Film	Art	Eat out
Overall	27.9	29.1	19.2	23.7
Axis 1	13.7	45.3	12.0	29.0
Axis 2	60.9	29.2	3.8	6.0

Figure 3.12 shows the 10 categories selected for the interpretation of specific axis 1. The sum of their contributions is 91%. This axis shows an opposition "hard" versus "soft," the same as that of axis 3 in the overall analysis. The correlation of the first specific variable on I' with the third principal variable restricted to I' is equal to .82.

Axis 2 is the specific axis of Television (61% of the variance of axis). It shows a clear-cut opposition between the 41 individuals who have chosen TV-Nature (top) and those who have chosen another type of program, especially TV-News (bottom).

Figure 3.13 shows the subcloud of the 183 individuals in specific plane 1-2.

To situate the subcloud in the whole cloud, we calculate the multiple correlation R of each specific variable on I' with the first three principal variables (of the global analysis) restricted to I': $R = .93$ for the first specific variable, $R = .40$ for the second one, and $R = .23$ for the third one.

Now, inspecting the subcloud, we study the *structuring factor Gender*, that is, the subcloud of 99 women and that of 84 men. The coordinates of the

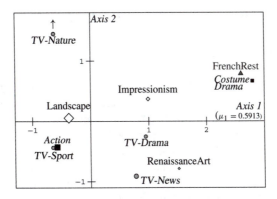

Figure 3.12 *Taste Example.* Cloud of the 10 categories selected for the interpretation of specific axis 1, in specific plane 1-2 (half size). (The coordinate of TV-Nature relative to axis 2 is equal to 2.75, hence the arrow.)

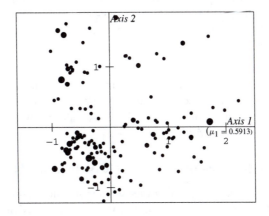

Figure 3.13 Cloud of the 183 individuals (55–64 age group) in the plane of the first two specific axes (halfsize).

mean points of the two subclouds are found to be -0.2897 (men) and 0.2458 (women), hence the calibrated deviation is $(0.2458 + 0.2897)/\sqrt{0.5913} = 0.70$, which is a notable deviation: Axis 1 is related to *Gender*.

Conclusion: For the 55-64 age group, the first cleavage, represented by the first axis, is close to that of the third axis of the overall analysis and is linked to Gender.

CHAPTER 4. STRUCTURED DATA ANALYSIS

The geometric modeling of an Individuals × Variables table may purposely leave aside some structures the basic sets are equipped with. Clearly, if we want to investigate the role of *Gender* on lifestyle, we had better *not* use *Gender* for constructing the space of lifestyle. By *structuring factors*, we mean descriptors of the two basic sets that have not served to define the distance between individuals; and by *structured data*, we designate data tables whose basic sets are equipped with structuring factors.[1] Clearly, structured data constitute the rule rather than the exception, leading to questions of interest that may be central to the study of the geometric model of data.

In conventional statistics, there are techniques for handling structuring factors, such as analysis of variance (ANOVA)—including multivariate analysis of variance (MANOVA) extensions—and regression; by *structured data analysis* we mean the integration of such techniques into GDA, while preserving the GDA construction.

Plan of Chapter 4. We first discuss supplementary variables versus structuring factors (Section 4.1), then experimental versus observational data (Section 4.2). We introduce concentration ellipses (Section 4.3). We illustrate Structured Data Analysis on the Taste Example, studying in depth the crossing of *Gender* and *Age* (Section 4.4).

4.1 From Supplementary Variables to Structuring Factors

As a matter of fact, there is a GDA technique for handling structured data, namely that of *supplementary variables*. We have illustrated this technique in the preceding section (Section 3.2, p. 46). GDA users have widely applied this technique; for instance, in *La Distinction* (1979), Bourdieu puts age, father's profession, education level, and income as supplementary variables to explain differences in lifestyle.

In our view, the technique of supplementary variables constitutes a first step toward structured data analysis. The limitations of this technique become apparent when considering that supplementary category amounts to confining attention to a mean point of a subcloud of individuals (fundamental property of MCA), ignoring the dispersion of the subcloud. Thus, in *La Distinction*, this concern led Bourdieu to stylize class fractions—"the

---

[1] "Structuring factors" have nothing to do with principal variables, often called "factors."

most powerful explanatory factor," as he put it—as contours in the space of individuals, very much in the spirit of structured data analysis (see Rouanet et al., 2000). In our recent work, the subclouds generated by structuring factors are summarized by concentration ellipses.[2]

4.2 From Experimental to Observational Data

In the experimental paradigm, there is a clear-cut distinction between *experimental factors* (under experimenter's control), alias independent variables, and *dependent variables*. There is a *factorial design* expressing the relations between factors such as nesting and crossing. Statistical analysis aims at studying the *effects of factors* in the framework of the design: main effects, between-effects, within-effects, and interaction effects.

In observational data, principal clouds may be taken as dependent variables, and similar relationships between structuring factors may also be expressed and studied. Two provisos, however, are in order: (1) Since structuring factors are not experimentally controlled, the notion of effect is usually metaphorical, and (2) while experimental designs are usually balanced by construction, structuring factors in observational data happen to be more or less *correlated*; hence, the definitions of the various effects of factors require more elaboration.

Given a partition of a cloud of individuals, the mean points of the subclouds (category mean points) define a derived cloud, whose variance is called the *between-variance* of the partition. The weighted average of the variances of subclouds is called the *within-variance* of the partition. The overall variance of the cloud breaks down additively into between-variance plus within-variance (Section 2.3, p. 20).

Given a set of factors and of principal clouds, the *breakdown of variances* consists in calculating the variances of various effects on each principal cloud.

4.3 Concentration Ellipses

Geometric summaries of subclouds in a principal plane are provided by *concentration ellipses*. By definition (see Cramér, 1946, p. 283), the concentration ellipse of a subcloud is the ellipse of inertia (see infra) such that a uniform distribution over the interior of the ellipse has the same variance as the subcloud; this definition leads to the ellipse with semi-axes $(2\gamma_1, 2\gamma_2)$, where $(\gamma_1)^2$ and $(\gamma_2)^2$ are the eigenvalues associated with the principal axes

---

[2] For instance, in the study of the French political space by Chiche, Le Roux, Perrineau, and Rouanet (2000), we constructed the concentration ellipses for various electorates.

of the subcloud. For a normally shaped subcloud, the concentration ellipse contains 86.47% of the points of the subcloud.

Target Example. We exemplify the concept on the subcloud C of the 10-point cloud presented in Section 2.2 (p. 16).

From the principal coordinates of the cloud of 10 points (Table 2.3, p. 30), one gets the coordinates of the mean point C of the subcloud C ($m_1 = +3.8333$, $m_2 = -1.2778$), as well as its variances ($v_1 = 25.30612$, $v_2 = 21.22449$), and covariance ($c = +7.75510$). Applying the formulas on page 32, eigenvalues are given by $\frac{46.5306}{2} \pm \frac{1}{2}\sqrt{(4.0816)^2 + 4 \times (7.75510)^2}$, hence $(\gamma_1)^2 = 31.2844 = (5.5932)^2$ and $(\gamma_2)^2 = (3.9046)^2$; one has $\tan \alpha_1 = \left((\gamma_1)^2 - v_1\right)/c = (31.2844 - 25.30612)/7.75510 = 0.7709$, hence $\alpha_1 = 37.63°$. The concentration ellipse of the subcloud C has semi-axes $2\gamma_1 = 11.19$ and $2\gamma_2 = 7.81$, and the angle between its major axis and the first principal axis of the cloud of 10 points is $\alpha_1 = 37.63°$ (Figure 4.1).

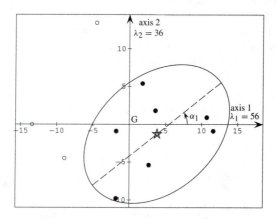

Figure 4.1 *Target Example.* Representation of subcloud C (7 black points) in the principal axes of the 10-point cloud; concentration ellipse of subcloud C with its major axis (dashed line) and mean point ($\star$).

Ellipses of inertia. The ellipses of inertia of a cloud have their center at the mean point of the cloud and are homothetic with one another. Relative to any orthonormal basis, the ellipse of index κ (read "kappa") has the equation:

$$\frac{v_2(y_1 - m_1)^2 - 2c(y_1 - m_1)(y_2 - m_2) + v_1(y_2 - m_2)^2}{v_1 v_2 - c^2} = \kappa^2.$$

For $\kappa = 1$, the ellipse of inertia is the classic *indicator ellipse*. The concentration ellipse corresponds to $\kappa = 2$. In GDA, concentration ellipses provide geometric summaries of subclouds induced by a structuring factor (or by a clustering procedure), as illustrated hereafter (Section 4.4). More precisely, they are the geometrical representations of the concentration of the points of the subclouds around their mean points.

Remark. In statistical inference, under an appropriate modeling, inertia ellipses also provide *confidence ellipses* for the true mean points of subclouds, as will be seen in Section 5.

4.4 Taste Example: Study of Gender and Age

We illustrate the approach of structured data analysis by studying the *Gender* and *Age* questions of the Taste Example, first separately and then jointly.

Study of Gender

Each gender determines a subcloud of the cloud of individuals. Relative to the principal axes, the coordinates of the mean points and the variances of the two subclouds are given in Table 4.1.

Table 4.1 *Taste Example: Gender.* Coordinates of the mean points and variances of the 2 subclouds of men and women on the first 3 axes; double breakdown of variances along axes and *Gender.*

Gender	weight	Mean point coordinates			Variances		
		Axis 1	Axis 2	Axis 3	Axis 1	Axis 2	Axis 3
men	513	−0.112	−0.158	+0.300	.2915	.2528	.2567
women	702	+0.082	+0.115	−0.219	.4639	.3916	.2613
				within–Gender	.3911	.3330	.2593
				between–Gender	.0092	.0182	.0657
				total (λ)	.4004	.3512	.3250

The deviations between the two mean points along the axes are $d_1 = -0.112 - 0.082 = -0.194$, $d_2 = -0.273$ and $d3 = +0.519$. If we scale these deviations by the standard deviation of axis ($\sqrt{\lambda}$), we get $d_1/\sqrt{0.4004} = -0.308$ (axis 1), $d_2/\sqrt{0.3512} = -0.461$ (axis 2), and $d_3/\sqrt{0.3250} = +0.910$ (axis 3). If a scaled deviation (in absolute value) greater than 0.5 is deemed to be *notable*, and a scaled deviation (in absolute value) greater than 1 is deemed to be *large*, one obtains the "rule of thumb"

72

stated in Section 3.2 (p. 46). Here only the deviation d_3 is notable, followed by d_2. Hence we will represent the two subclouds not only in plane 1-2 but also in plane 2-3 (Figures 4.2 and 4.3, p. 72).

In plane 1-2, there is a very large dispersion of the subcloud of women and no clear separation with the subcloud of men. In plane 2-3, the subcloud of women is less dispersed and its concentration ellipse is shifted toward "soft" tastes (bottom); the subcloud of men is much less dispersed, and its bulk lies in the North–West quadrant.

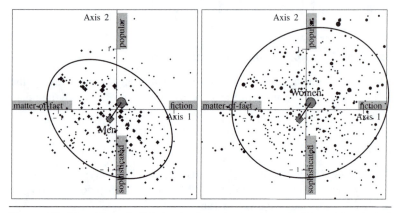

Figure 4.2 *Taste Example.* Subclouds of men (top) and women (bottom) in principal plane 1-2 with mean points and concentration ellipses (halfsize).

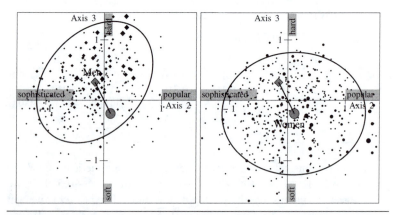

Figure 4.3 *Taste Example.* Subclouds of men (left) and women (right) in principal plane 2-3 with mean points and concentration ellipses (halfsize).

The double breakdown of variance along the axes and *Gender* shows the large dispersions of the subclouds (Table 4.1, p. 71). The η^2 coefficient (between/total ratio, see definition on page 22) is 1/5 on axis 3 and very small on axes 1 and 2.

To sum up, the differences in taste between genders are mainly on axis 3 ("hard" vs. "soft").

Study of Age

Each age group determines a subcloud of individuals with its mean point and its variances along the axes; hence, there are six subclouds. Table 4.2 gives, for the first three principal axes, the coordinates of the six mean points, the double breakdown of the variance according to the axes and *Age*, and the between and the within variances. The individual differences within age groups are large; η^2 is less than 1/5 on axis 1, much smaller on axis 2, and virtually null on axis 3.

Table 4.2 Coordinates of mean points, variances of the 6 age group subclouds on the first 3 axes; double breakdown of variance.

		Coordinates			Variances		
Age	weight	Axis 1	Axis 2	Axis 3	Axis 1	Axis 2	Axis 3
18-24	93	+0.589	−0.332	+0.014	.1916	.3946	.2581
25-34	248	+0.272	−0.191	−0.014	.3083	.3225	.2934
35-44	258	+0.089	−0.053	+0.052	.3371	.2880	.3406
45-54	191	−0.054	−0.070	−0.047	.3604	.3176	.3120
55-64	183	−0.367	+0.101	−0.013	.3121	.2459	.4095
$\geq$ 65	242	−0.281	+0.359	0.000	.3401	.3143	.3078
				within–Age	.3206	.3068	.3240
				between–Age	.0798	.0444	.0010
				total (λ)	.4004	.3512	.3250

Figure 4.4—a refinement of Figure 1.4 (p. 9)—shows the two subclouds of the 55-64 and $\geq$ 65 age groups and the two subclouds of the 18-24 and 25-34 age groups, together with their concentration ellipses.

The two subclouds of elderly people lie roughly in the North–West quadrant, with "matter-of-fact" and "popular" tastes. The 18-24 subcloud is markedly distinct. It has a small dispersion on axis 1 (variance = 0.1916) and "fiction" oriented tastes and a large dispersion on axis 2 (variance = 0.3946) with tastes ranging from "sophisticated" to rather "popular."

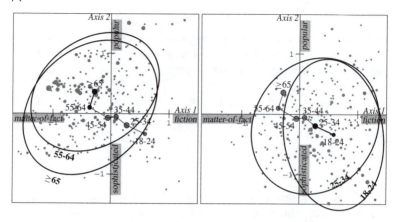

Figure 4.4 *Taste Example.* Subclouds of individuals of age groups 55–64 and ≥65 (top), and of age groups 18–24 and 25–34 (bottom), in principal plane 1-2, with concentration ellipses; mean points of the six age groups (half size).

Crossing of Age and Gender

In the cloud of individuals, the crossing of *Age* and *Gender* induces a cloud of $6 \times 2 = 12$ category mean points (Table 4.3 and Figure 4.5 [left]).

We will take this weighted cloud as the *basic data set* for the analyses that follow and call it the *Age × Gender* cloud.

From Table 4.3, one verifies that the mean point of the *Age × Gender* cloud is the mean point of the cloud of individuals, the variance on axis 1 is 0.0954, and that on axis 2 is 0.0631; hence the variance in plane 1-2, denoted by $V_{A \times G}$, is $0.0954 + 0.0632 = 0.1586$.

Table 4.3 *Taste Example:* Weights (n_k) and coordinates of the 12 *Age×Gender* mean points for axes 1 and 2, of the 6 *Age* mean points and of the 2 *Gender* mean points, already shown in Tables 4.1 &4.2.

Age×		men			women			Age	
Gender	n_k	Axis 1	Axis 2	n_k	Axis 1	Axis 2	n_k	Axis 1	Axis 2
18-24	40	+0.4267	−0.4043	53	+0.7121	−0.2781	93	+0.589	−0.332
25-34	106	+0.0792	−0.3904	142	+0.4163	−0.0417	248	+0.272	−0.191
35-44	117	−0.0799	−0.2130	141	+0.2292	+0.0792	258	+0.089	−0.053
45-54	74	−0.1273	−0.3049	117	−0.0073	+0.0791	191	−0.054	−0.070
55-64	84	−0.3055	+0.0185	99	−0.4188	+0.1711	183	−0.367	+0.101
≥65	92	−0.4209	+0.2452	150	−0.1945	+0.4282	242	−0.281	+0.359
Gender	513	−0.112	−0.158	702	+0.082	+0.115			

The mean point of the six age group points for men (♦ in Figure 4.5) is the mean point of the subcloud of men; it has coordinates $(-0.112, -0.158)$ (Tables 4.1 [p. 71] and 4.3). Similarly the mean point of the six age group points for women (● in Figure 4.5) has coordinates $(+0.082, +0.115)$, hence the *Gender* cloud of two points (♦, ●) shown in Figure 4.5 (right). The variance of the *Gender* cloud in plane 1-2 (between-*Gender* variance), denoted by V_G, is equal to $0.0092 + 0.0182 = 0.0274$ (Table 4.1, p. 71).

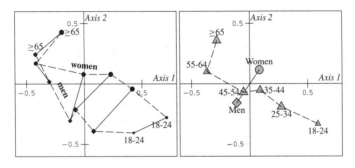

Figure 4.5   *Taste Example: Age* × *Gender* cloud (left), *Gender* and *Age* clouds (right) in plane 1–2 (same scale as Figure 1.3, p.8).

Similarly, we get the *Age* cloud consisting of the six mean points of the two gender points for each age (▲ in Figure 4.5). Its variance in plane 1-2 (between-*Age* variance), denoted by V_A, is equal to $0.0798 + 0.0444 = 0.1242$ (Table 4.2, p. 73).

Observe the (expected) resemblance between Figure 4.5 and Figure 3.9 (p. 60). Figure 4.5 depicts the *Age* and *Gender* category mean points in the cloud of individuals, while Figure 3.9 depicts the *Age* and *Gender* category points in the cloud of categories.

Main effect and within-effect of gender.   For *Gender*, one has $2 - 1 = 1$ degree of freedom. The geometric vector joining the two gender points defines the *main effect* of *Gender* (Figure 4.6, p. 76); its coordinates are $(-0.194, -0.273)$ in plane 1-2 (already found, p. 71). Figure 4.6 (left) shows the six subclouds of two gender points. For each age group, the vector joining the two gender points defines the effect of *Gender* within-age group: For the 18-24 age group, the *vector-effect* of *Gender* has coordinates $+0.427 - 0.712 = -0.285$ on axis 1 and $+0.126$ on axis 2. The effects of *Gender* within-*Age* is defined by the six vector-effects.

From Table 4.3 (p. 74), one calculates the variances of the six subclouds of two points (Table 4.4). For instance, for the 18–24 age group, the variance

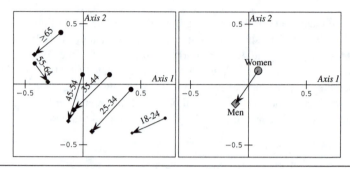

Figure 4.6 *Taste example.* Six within-effects (vectors) of *Gender* for each age group (left) and main effect (vector) of *Gender* (right) in plane 1-2.

along axis 1 is $\frac{40}{93} \times \frac{53}{93}(0.4267 - 0.7121)^2 = 0.0200$ (see the formula on p. 23). The weighted mean of the variances of the six subclouds is the variance of *Gender* within-*Age*. It is denoted by $V_{G\text{within}A}$, and is equal to 0.0345.

Table 4.4 Variances of the 2–point subclouds on axes 1 and 2, in plane 1-2.

Age	18-24	25-34	35-44	45-54	55-64	≥65
Axis 1	0.0200	0.0278	0.0237	0.0034	0.0032	0.0121
Axis 2	0.0039	0.0298	0.0212	0.0350	0.0058	0.0079
Plane 1-2	0.0239	0.0576	0.0448	0.0384	0.0090	0.0200
weights	93	248	258	191	183	242

Main effects and within-effects of age. For *Age*, one has $6 - 1 = 5$ degrees of freedom. The vector joining the two points (18-24, 25-34) defines the main effect of *Age* for these two classes. Its coordinates are $+0.589 - 0.272 = 0.317$ (axis 1) and $-0.332 + 0.191 = -0.141$ (axis 2). Figure 4.7 shows the five vectors representing the *main effects* of *Age* (right) and the five vectors representing the *within-effects* for each gender (left), that is, the effects of *Age* within-*Gender*.

From Table 4.3 (p. 74), one calculates the variances of the subclouds of six age group points for the two genders; that is, $0.05369 + 0.05395 = 0.10764$ (men) and $0.10995 + 0.03851 = 0.14846$ (women) in plane 1-2. The weighted mean of the two variances is the variance of *Age* within-*Gender*. It is denoted by $V_{A\text{within}G}$ and equal to $(513 \times 0.10764 + 702 \times 0.14846)/1215 = 0.13123$.

Interaction and additive cloud. The six *Gender* vector-effects (Figure 4.6, left) differ from one age group to another; that is, the within-effects of *Gender* are not the same for the different age groups. Equivalently,

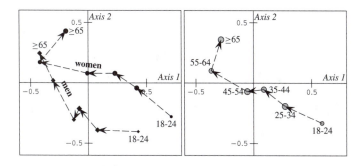

Figure 4.7 *Taste Example.* Five successive within-effects (vectors) of *Age* for each gender (left) and main effects (vectors) of *Age* (right) in plane 1-2.

the *Age* vector-effects differ between genders; that is, the within-effects of *Age* are not the same for men and women (Figure 4.7). In such a situation, it is commonly said that there is an *interaction* effect[3] between the two factors.

A cloud on the crossing of two factors can be fitted by an *additive cloud*, that is, a cloud without interaction, with the same derived clouds on each factor as the cloud on the crossing. Figure 4.8 depicts the additive cloud in plane 1-2 fitted to the *Age* × *Gender* cloud[4] whose derived clouds are the *Gender* and *Age* clouds depicted in Figure 4.5 (p. 75).

In the additive cloud, by construction, the within-effects for each factor are equal to one another. For instance, the six *Gender* vector-effects have the same coordinates $(-0.203, -0.263)$. This vector-effect can be taken as the *averaged within-effect* of *Gender* within-*Age* in the *Gender* × *Age* cloud, and similarly for the effects of *Age* within-*Gender*. In plane 1-2, the variance of the additive cloud is $0.08979 + 0.06115 = 0.15094$.[5]

Structure effect. The average within-effect of *Gender* (as it appears in the additive cloud) is the vector with coordinates $(-0.203, -0.263)$; the main effect of *Gender* is the vector with coordinates $(-0.194, -0.273)$. The two effects are not far away. This is because the factors *Gender* and *Age* are weakly correlated; that is, the *Gender* ratios vary little among age groups. For the same reason, the within-effects of *Age* are not far from the main effects of *Age*.

---

[3] Again, the term *interaction* is metaphorical and does not imply any substantive interplay between *Age* and *Gender*.

[4] For the construction of the additive cloud, see the note on p. 79.

[5] For the calculation of variance, see p. 80.

78

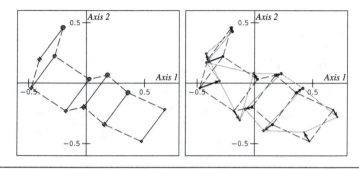

Figure 4.8 *Additive* cloud fitted to the *Gender* × *Age* cloud (left) and the 12 deviations (vectors) from the *Gender* × *Age* cloud (right).

When factors are strongly correlated, however, the within-effects of one factor may greatly differ from the main effects of this factor, or even have opposite signs; in this case, we say that there is a *structure effect*.

Structure effect and interaction are two different things. In our example, there is some interaction yet hardly any structure effect. The opposite can also occur: no interaction but structure effect. The procedures presented in this section hold for the general case involving both structure effect and interaction.

Breakdowns of variance. There are three additive breakdowns of the variance of the *Gender* × *Age* cloud (Table 4.5): (between-genders) + (*Age* within-*Gender*); (between-ages) + (*Gender* within-*Age*); and (additive) + (interaction).

Table 4.5 Three additive breakdowns of variances of the *Age* × *Gender* cloud and variances of the *Age* × *Gender* cloud, for axis 1, axis 2 and plane 1-2.

	between genders	*Age* within– *Gender*	between ages	*Gender* within– *Age*	additive	inter- action	*Age* × *Gender*
Axis 1	0.0092	0.0862	0.0798	0.0157	0.0898	0.0056	0.0954
Axis 2	0.0182	0.0450	0.0444	0.0188	0.0611	0.0021	0.0632
Plane 1-2	0.0274	0.1312	0.1242	0.0345	0.1509	0.0077	0.1586

Interaction, however weak, is revealed by the fact that the variance of the additive cloud (0.1509) is smaller than the variance of *Gender* × *Age* cloud (0.1586). Low correlation between factors is revealed by the fact that

$V_G(0.0274)$ is not far from $V_{G\text{within}A}$ (0.034), that V_A (0.1242) is not far from $V_{A\text{within}G}$ (0.131), and that the variance of the additive cloud (0.1509) is close to the sum of the between-variances ($V_G + V_A = 0.1516$).

Note on the determination of the additive cloud. The additive cloud can be obtained by proceeding to two weighted linear regressions, one for each axis, with the weights of the crossing *Age×Gender* (Table 4.3, p. 74). For each regression, the independent variables are the indicator variables of the categories of the two factors; the dependent variables are the first and the second principal variables. The results of the two regressions are given in Table 4.6.

Table 4.6 Regression coefficients of the principal variables 1 and 2 on the indicator variables of *Gender* and *Age*, taking Women and the 18–24 age group as references; and R^2 (squared multiple correlations).

	constant	men	25-34	35-44	45-54	55-65	>65	R^2
Axis 1	+.6766	−.2030	−.3177	−.4956	−.6518	−.9502	−.8800	0.9409
Axis 2	−.2194	−.2625	+.1409	+.2852	+.2515	+.4410	+.6779	0.9674

The coordinates of the additive cloud are the predicted values of the regression. They can be obtained as follows.

1. Starting with the reference point (18–24, women) ($\star$) with coordinates (+0.6766,−0.2194), we get the point (18–24, men) by adding the coefficients of men to these two coordinates, that is, +0.6766 − 0.2030 = +0.4736 and −0.2194 − 0.2625 = −0.4819.

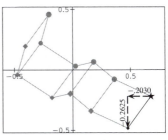

2. From the regression coefficients of the 25–34 category, one constructs the point (25–34, women) with coordinates +0.6766 − 0.3177 = +0.3589 and −0.2194 + 0.1409 = −0.0785.

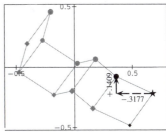

3. From the regression coefficients of the 35–44 category, one constructs the point (35–44, men) with coordinates $+0.6766 - 0.4956 = +0.1810$, and $-0.2194 + 0.2852 = +0.0658$, and so on.

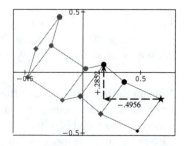

The variance of the additive cloud is obtained by multiplying each R^2 coefficient (Table 4.6, p. 79) by the corresponding variance of the *Age* × *Gender* cloud (Table 4.5, p. 78), that is, $0.9409 \times 0.0954 = 0.0898$ (axis 1) and $0.9674 \times 0.0632 = 0.0611$ (axis 2).

CHAPTER 5. INDUCTIVE DATA ANALYSIS

Far better an approximate answer to the right question ...
than an exact answer to the wrong one.

—*J. Tukey*

In many studies, researchers would like to draw conclusions that go beyond the particular data set under study. With small data sets, however, such conclusions may be precarious, and this is what motivates researchers to resort to the formal procedures traditionally called *statistical inference.* Indeed, statistical inference could and should be used more liberally in GDA—especially in MCA—provided that it is performed in the line of inductive data analysis (IDA).

Descriptive versus inductive procedures. So far in this book, we have only dealt with descriptive procedures. What exactly is meant by "descriptive" procedures? There is a clear-cut operational response to this question. Descriptive procedures *do not depend* on sample size, that is, they can be based only on relative frequencies. In contrast, inference procedures *do depend* on sample size.

Descriptive statistics are the statistics produced by descriptive procedures. Examples are the mean, the variance, and the correlation coefficient. For a contingency table, the formula $\chi^2 = n\,\Phi^2$ relates the mean square contingency coefficient Φ^2, which is a descriptive statistic, to the test statistic χ^2, which is not a descriptive statistic. If the absolute frequencies of the table are all duplicated, Φ^2 is invariant, whereas χ^2 is multiplied by 2 and consequently (for a nonzero association) becomes more significant. The paradigm

$$\text{test statistic} = \text{sample size} \times \text{descriptive statistic}$$

provides the general key for articulating inference procedures with descriptive ones. All statistical methods produce descriptive statistics that can be combined with sample size to yield inductive procedures.

Inductive data analysis. In a research study, the IDA phase will aim at substantiating descriptive conclusions (whenever possible), allowing for noncontrolled sources of variation:

$$\text{Description first, inference later!}$$

For instance, we have found that the mean point of Indians (p. 58) is far from the center of the cloud, on the "fiction-sophisticated" quadrant. This finding triggers the natural query from the researcher (informally stated): Is the observed deviation a genuine one, or might it be due to chance? To cope with this query, the usual sampling models, with their drastic assumptions, are simply not appropriate. The *combinatorial framework*, which is entirely free from assumptions, is the most in harmony with IDA. The typicality problem is a case in point.

The typicality problem. The question about the Indians' group can be reformulated as follows: "Can the Indians' group be assimilated to the reference population, or is it atypical of it?" The basic idea of the solution is to compare the group of interest with size n with the subsets of the reference population with the same size n. Thus, a set of possible subclouds is generated; the proportion of possible subclouds whose mean points are more extreme than (or as extreme as) the observed mean point is called the *combinatorial observed level* (alias combinatorial p-value) and defines the *degree of typicality* of the group mean point. A low p-value will be declared statistically significant in a combinatorial sense[1] and will point to a genuine effect, presumably "not due to chance."

Remark. In IDA, looking at the importance of effect is done at the descriptive analysis stage, not as an afterthought following significance testing. As a consequence, if significance testing is performed as a follow-up of the conclusion of a descriptive important effect (*safety rule*), no seeming "conflict" between a significant though unimportant effect can happen.

Plan of Chapter 5. We present the typicality test for the mean point of a subcloud with respect to the overall cloud of individuals (Section 5.1). Then we present the homogeneity test for the mean points of two subclouds (Section 5.2). Then we outline confidence ellipses (Section 5.3). Illustrations are taken from the Taste Example.

The typicality test and the homogeneity test presented in this section are developed in detail in Chapters 8 and 9 of the book by Le Roux and Rouanet (2004). These two tests are *permutation tests*. Permutation tests were initiated by Fisher and Pitman in the 1930s.

5.1 Typicality Tests

We will study the typicality of a subcloud of n individuals with respect to the overall cloud of N individuals. The set of the N individuals is

---

[1] This combinatorial conception of significance level exactly corresponds to the "nonstochastic interpretation" presented by Freedman and Lane (1983).

taken as a *reference population*, and an n-element subset of the reference population is a *sample*. The set of all n-element subsets[2] defines the *sample space*. With each sample is associated a possible subcloud, hence $\binom{N}{n}$ possible subclouds. To characterize the typicality, we take a test statistic. The distribution of the $\binom{N}{n}$ values of the test statistic for each possible subcloud is called the *sampling distribution* of the test statistic. Then the proportion of the possible subclouds for which the value of the test statistic is more extreme than (or equal to) the observed value (value of the test statistic for the subcloud under study) defines the *combinatorial observed level* (p-value).

Hereafter we study the typicality test for comparing the mean point of a subcloud with the reference mean point (the mean point of the overall cloud), first for a principal axis then for a principal plane.

Typicality for a principal axis

For a principal axis of variance λ, with each possible subcloud is associated the coordinate $\bar{y}$ of its mean point—hence the *sampling distribution* of $\bar{y}$. The mean of the sampling distribution is 0 and its variance, denoted by V, is

$$V = \frac{1}{n} \frac{N-n}{N-1} \lambda$$

(a classical formula in finite sampling). When n is not small (and far from N), the sampling distribution will be fitted by a normal distribution with mean 0 and variance V. Hence the test statistic

$$Z = \frac{\bar{y}}{\sqrt{V}} = \sqrt{n \frac{N-1}{N-n}} \frac{\bar{y}}{\sqrt{\lambda}},$$

which is approximately distributed as a standard normal variable. Let z_{obs} be the observed value of the test statistic Z, that is, its value for the subcloud under study; the approximate p-value is denoted by $\tilde{p}$.

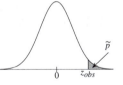

Taste example: *The Young (18-24) subcloud on axis 1* ($n = 93$, $\lambda_1 = 0.4004$).

---

[2] Recall that the number of ways of selecting n elements out of N is the binomial coefficient

$$\binom{N}{n} = \frac{N(N-1)\dots(N-n+1)}{n(n-1)\dots \times 2 \times 1}.$$

From Table 4.2 (p. 73), one gets the coordinate of the mean point of the Young subcloud, that is, $\bar{y} = +0.589$, hence the scaled deviation[3] $y = +0.589/\sqrt{0.4004} = +0.931$. Descriptively, the deviation is notable. One has $N = 1215, n = 93$, hence

$$z_{obs} = \sqrt{93 \times \frac{1215 - 1}{1215 - 93}} \times (+0.931) = 100.63 \times (+0.931) = +9.34$$

and $\tilde{p} = 0.000$ (rounding to three decimal places). This result is highly significant.[4]

Conclusion. For the mean on axis 1, the Young subcloud is atypical of the overall cloud of individuals, on the "fiction" side (at the one-sided level .005).

Taste example: *The Indians' subcloud on axis 1* $(n = 38)$. The coordinate of the mean point of the Indians' subcloud is $\bar{y} = +0.316$ (see Section 3, p. 58), hence the scaled deviation $+0.316/\sqrt{0.4004} = +0.50$. Descriptively, the deviation is notable.
One has

$$z_{obs} = \sqrt{38 \times \frac{1215 - 1}{1215 - 38}} \times (+0.50) = \sqrt{39.19} \times (+0.50) = +3.1 (> 2.58)$$

and $\tilde{p} = 0.001$, a significant result.

Conclusion: For the mean point on axis 1, the Indians' subcloud is atypical of the overall cloud, on the "fiction" side (at the one-sided level .005).

Typicality for a principal plane

The typicality test can be extended to two or more dimensions.

For two dimensions, denoting $(\bar{y}_1, \bar{y}_2)$ the coordinates of the mean point of the subcloud, we take

$$d = \sqrt{\left(\frac{\bar{y}_1}{\sqrt{\lambda_1}}\right)^2 + \left(\frac{\bar{y}_2}{\sqrt{\lambda_2}}\right)^2} = \sqrt{y_1^2 + y_2^2},$$

as an importance index of the deviation from the mean point of the subcloud to the mean point G of the overall cloud. Hence, the test statistic

---

[3] Recall that the scaled deviation $\bar{y}/\sqrt{\lambda} = y$ is the importance index defined in Section 4 (p. 72).

[4] The value 9.34 is much larger than 2.58, the critical value of the standard normal variable at the conventional two-sided level $\alpha = .01$, that is, at the one-sided level .005.

$$X^2 = n\frac{N-1}{N-n}d^2,$$

whose sampling distribution is approximately χ^2 with 2 degrees of freedom (df).

Taste example: *The Young subcloud in plane 1-2* ($\lambda_1 = 0.4004$, $\lambda_2 = 0.3512$). From Table 4.2 (p. 73), one gets $\bar{y}_1 = +0.589$ and $\bar{y}_2 = -0.332$. One has

$$d = \sqrt{\frac{(0.589)^2}{0.4004} + \frac{(-0.332)^2}{0.3512}} = \sqrt{1.180} = 1.09.$$

Descriptively the deviation is large.

The observed value of the test statistic is $X^2_{obs} = 100.63 \times 1.180 = 118.74$; hence $\tilde{p} = 0.000$, a highly significant result.[5]

Conclusion: For the mean point in plane 1-2, the Young subcloud is *atypical* of the overall cloud, on the side of the "fiction–sophisticated" quadrant (at two-sided level .001).

Taste example: *The Indians' subcloud in plane 1-2.* The coordinates of the mean point of the Indians' subcloud are $(+0.316, -0.343)$ (Section 3, p. 58). One has

$$d = \sqrt{\frac{0.316^2}{0.400} + \frac{(-0.343)^2}{0.351}} = \sqrt{0.58} = 0.76.$$

Descriptively the deviation is notable.

One has $X^2_{obs} = 39.19 \times 0.58 = 22.92$, a highly significant result.

Conclusion: For the mean point in plane 1-2, the Indians' subcloud is *atypical* of the overall cloud, on the side of the "fiction-sophisticated" quadrant (at the two-sided level .001).

5.2 Homogeneity Tests

The homogeneity test is the combinatorial procedure that aims at comparing several groups of individuals. Let us consider two disjoint subsets of individuals with sizes n_1 and n_2 (with $n = n_1 + n_2$), and the set of the $N!/(n_1!n_2!(N-n)!)$ possible pairs of disjoint subsets with sizes (n_1, n_2), hence the associated set of possible pairs of subclouds. To characterize the homogeneity of two subclouds, we consider the deviation between their mean points and take a test statistic. The distribution of the $N!/(n_1!n_2!(N-n)!)$ values of the test statistic for each possible pair of

---

[5] $X^2_{obs} = 118.74$ is much larger than 9.21, the critical value of χ^2 with 2 df for $\alpha = .001$.

subclouds defines the *permutation distribution* of the test statistic. The proportion of possible pairs for which the value of the test statistic is more extreme than (or equal to) the observed value defines the observed level (*p*-value).

Hereafter we study the homogeneity test for comparing the two mean points of subclouds associated with two groups, for a principal axis and for a principal plane.

Homogeneity test for a principal axis

For a pair of subclouds, we consider the deviation between their mean points, that is, the difference $\overline{d}$ of the coordinates of their mean points on the principal axis. With each possible pair of subclouds there is attached a mean difference $\overline{d}$, hence the permutation distribution of $\overline{d}$.

For a principal axis of variance λ, the mean of the permutation distribution of $\overline{d}$ is 0 and the variance, denoted by V, is

$$V = \frac{N}{N-1} \frac{\lambda}{\widetilde{n}}, \text{ with } \widetilde{n} = \frac{1}{\frac{1}{n_1} + \frac{1}{n_2}}.$$

The permutation distribution will be fitted by a normal distribution with mean 0 and variance V. One considers the test statistic

$$Z = \frac{\overline{d}}{\sqrt{V}} = \sqrt{\widetilde{n}} \sqrt{\frac{N-1}{N}} \, d$$

(with $d = \overline{d}/\sqrt{\lambda}$), which is approximately distributed as a standard normal variable, hence $\widetilde{p}$.

Taste example: *Comparing two age-group subclouds of women on axis 1.* The two age groups are the 25–34 and the 55–64 ones, with sizes $n_1 = 142$ and $n_2 = 99$. The coordinates of the mean points on axis 1 are $+0.4163$ and -0.4188 (Table 4.3, p. 74). Hence, the deviation $\overline{d}_1 = 0.4163 - (-0.4188) = 0.8351$ and the scaled deviation $d_1 = \overline{d}_1/\sqrt{\lambda_1} = 0.8351/\sqrt{0.4004} = 1.32$. Descriptively the deviation is important.

One has

$$\widetilde{n} = \frac{1}{\frac{1}{142} + \frac{1}{99}} = 58.332, \text{ hence } Z_{obs} = \sqrt{58.332} \times \sqrt{\frac{1214}{1215}} \times 1.32 = 10.07$$

and $\widetilde{p} = 0.000$, a highly significant result.

Remarks

1. If the two subclouds define a partition of the overall cloud, the homogenity test of the two subclouds is equivalent to the typicality test of one of the two subclouds.

2. Let $\cos\theta$ be the cosine of the angle between the line joining the two category points and the principal axis, in the cloud of categories. We have $Z = \sqrt{N-1}\cos\theta$.

3. The homogeneity test can be generalized to the K_q subclouds associated with a question q, taking the test statistic $X^2 = (N-1)\eta_q^2$, which is approximately distributed as χ^2 with $(K_q - 1)$ *df* (for the definition of η_q^2, see p. 22).

Homogeneity test for a principal plane

The homogeneity test can be extended to two or more dimensions.

For two dimensions, one takes as an importance index of the deviation between two mean points

$$D^2 = \frac{(\bar{d}_1)^2}{\lambda_1} + \frac{(\bar{d}_2)^2}{\lambda_2} = d_1^2 + d_2^2,$$

where $\bar{d}_1$ and $\bar{d}_2$ are, respectively, the differences between the coordinates of the two mean points on axis 1 and on axis 2. Hence the test statistic

$$X^2 = \tilde{n}\, \frac{N-1}{N}\, D^2,$$

whose distribution is approximately χ^2 with 2 *df*.

Taste example: *Comparing two age group subclouds of women in plane 1-2.* The two age groups are 25–34 and 55–64. One has $\bar{d}_1 = 0.4163 + 0.4188 = 0.8351$ and $\bar{d}_2 = 0.0417 + 0.1711 = 0.2128$, hence

$$D_{obs}^2 = (0.8351^2/0.40036) + (0.2128^2/0.35117) = 1.8709 = (1.37)^2.$$

Descriptively the deviation is important.

$X_{obs}^2 = 58.332 \times \frac{1214}{1215} \times 1.8709 = 109.04$, a highly significant result.

Comments on combinatorial inference

1. The typicality test applies to a subset of a data set (e.g., the Young) as well as to an external set (e.g., the Indians). In both cases, we wonder whether the group of interest can be assimilated to a random sample of the reference population.

2. The typicality and homogeneity tests depend on the data size, and are performed on *possible* data sets, not just on the data set itself; therefore, the procedure is inductive in character. A significant result will be naturally interpreted as a *genuine effect* that calls for a substantive interpretation.

3. For subclouds defined by a category (e.g., the Young), the typicality test on an axis amounts to the technique of *test values*, familiar to GDA users (Lebart et al., 1984, pp. 23–26). For a category k and axis ℓ, the observed value of the test statistic is $Z_{obs} = \sqrt{N-1} \cos \theta_{k\ell}$, where $\cos^2 \theta_{k\ell}$ is the quality of representation of category point M^k on axis ℓ (see the definition on p. 41).

4. The typicality tests presented above are tests with respect to a *reference population*. Other variants of combinatorial tests can be devised, such as typicality with respect to a *reference point* (Le Roux & Rouanet, 2004, p. 326).

5. The familiar nonparametric tests, such as the sign test, rank tests, Fisher's exact test for a 2×2 table, and so on are variants of permutation tests, for which explicit formulas can be derived and tables can be constructed. This rendered such tests applicable before the computer era. In contrast, for the basic Fisher–Pitman tests, a considerable amount of computation is required, even for fairly small sample sizes. This problem of computation, which long hindered the full use of permutation tests, has now been overcome.[6]

6. Permutation tests applied to situations with random allocation of units to treatments or groups are called *randomization tests* (see Edgington & Onghena, 2007, especially Section 1.11).

7. The normal model procedures (Student test, Hotelling test, etc.) can be performed whenever applicable. They usually lead to results of the same order of magnitude as the combinatorial procedures, even though they tend to be less conservative; that is, they are prone to producing more significant results.

---

[6] For small data sets, exact computations can be carried out. For intermediate sizes, Monte Carlo procedures can be used, that is, the p-value is calculated from a random sample of all possible data permutations. For large data sets, approximate methods involving classical distributions are often available.

5.3 Confidence Ellipses

Also motivated by the precariousness of the inductive conclusions drawn from small data sets, there is another natural query (again informally stated about the Indians' mean point): How does the "true" Indians' mean point differ from the observed mean point? The answer is provided by constructing a *confidence zone* around the observed mean point.

If we choose a conventional level α, a $(1 - \alpha)$ confidence zone is defined as the set of possible mean points that are not significantly different from the observed mean point. In the usual normal theory, the confidence zone in a plane is the κ_α-inertia ellipse of the subcloud (see Section 4.3, p. 69), such that $\kappa_\alpha^2 = \chi_\alpha^2/n$, where χ_α^2 is the critical value of the χ^2 distribution with 2 df at level α. For $\alpha = .05$, $\chi_\alpha^2 = 5.9915$.

Taste example: *Confidence ellipses for Indians and the Young.*

The 95% confidence ellipse of the Indians' mean point in plane 1-2 is such that $\kappa_\alpha^2 = \frac{5.9915}{38} = 0.158$ and $\kappa_\alpha = 0.40$ (see Figure 5.1, left).

For the Young, one has $\kappa_\alpha^2 = \frac{5.9915}{93} = 0.064$ and $\kappa_\alpha = 0.25$ (see Figure 5.1, right).

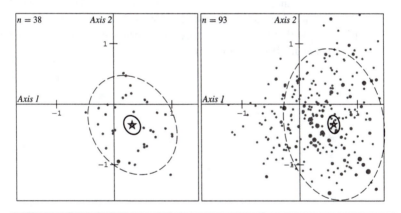

Figure 5.1 *Taste Example.* Concentration ellipse ($\kappa = 2$, dashed) and 95% confidence ellipse (under the normal theory) for the mean points ($\star$) of the Indians' subcloud (left) and the Young (right), in plane 1-2 (half scale).

Comments

1. The confidence ellipse for the mean point—a geometric inductive summary for the mean point—should not be confused with the concentration ellipse of the subcloud, a descriptive summary for the

subcloud. For moderate n, at usual α levels, the confidence ellipse is much smaller than the concentration one (Figure 5.1, p. 89).

2. Associated with the typicality test with respect to a reference point (see Comment 4 on page 88), there is a $(1 - \alpha)$ confidence ellipse, which is the κ_α-inertia ellipse with

$$\kappa_\alpha^2 = \frac{\chi_\alpha^2/n}{1 - \chi_\alpha^2/n},$$

slightly larger (i.e., more conservative) than that of the normal theory. For $\alpha = .05$, $\chi_\alpha^2 = 5.9915$.

For the Young ($n = 93$), one has $\kappa_\alpha^2 = 0.26$ (> 0.25), and for the Indians ($n = 38$), one has $\kappa_\alpha^2 = 0.43$ (> 0.40). Thus, in these two frameworks, the family of inertia ellipses, which provides geometric *descriptive* summaries of the *subcloud*, also provides geometric *inductive* summaries for the *mean point* of the subcloud.

3. In the *Bayesian framework*, assuming a *locally uniform prior*, the $1 - \alpha$ confidence ellipse becomes the $1 - \alpha$ highest density zone of the posterior distribution: The Bayesian probability that the true mean point lies within the $1 - \alpha$ confidence ellipse is equal to $1 - \alpha$ (see Rouanet et al., 1998, Chapter 7).

CHAPTER 6. FULL-SCALE RESEARCH STUDIES

The Taste Example with only four questions is by no means a research on lifestyle in the United Kingdom. The full-scale study (Le Roux et al., 2008) involved 41 questions, 17 regarding participation and 24 on taste, generating 166 active categories, allowing us to delineate and differentiate individuals. Indeed, the sequence of steps is very much the same as the one presented in Section 3, but the phase of coding data is crucial for providing meaningful results.

Different types of coding are used in MCA: pooling categories, dichotomous encoding, splitting quantitative variables, and so on (Section 6.2). More complex codings are involved in the construction of indices of importance (Section 6.1).

The set of variables can also be structured, or even constructed; for instance, in the study on gifted students (EPGY) conducted in cooperation with P. Suppes (Stanford University), the variables are built from the crossing of "teaching matters" and "types of performance" (Le Roux & Rouanet, 2003, 2004).

In this chapter, we outline the MCAs of two full-scale research studies. For each data set, we briefly present the *coding phase*, then we summarize the *statistical interpretation* (interpreting axes and structured data analysis).

Let us emphasize that the statistical interpretation should precede and substantiate the *sociological interpretation*.

Plan of Chapter 6. We sketch the MCA done in the study of "The Field of Publishers in France" (Bourdieu, 1999) (Section 6.1). Then we present the MCA done on "The Norwegian Field of Power" in the article by Hjellbrekke et al. (2007) (Section 6.2).

6.1 The Field of Publishers in France

The article "Une révolution conservatrice dans l'édition" is the last empirically based research done by P. Bourdieu (1999). Here, we summarize the salient features of the data coding and the analysis, in which we were actively involved.

Data Set and Coding

In this study, the "individuals" are 56 publishing companies that published literature, either written in or translated into French, between July 1995 and July 1996, excluding those that specialized in reissues (paperbacks, book club editions, etc.). The data are from several sources: bibliographies, archives, or the publishers themselves; 16 variables grouped under five headings were chosen to construct the "French publishing" geometric space.

1. *Legal and financial status* (3 variables)

    (1) Legal status in three categories: incorporated company ($n = 24$), limited liability company ($n = 23$), other ($n = 9$);

    (2) size index based on the firm capital, the turnover and the number of managers with five categories in ascending order of magnitude from "Size1" to "Size5" ($n = 14, 12, 12, 8, 6$) + unknown ($n = 4$);

    (3) number of employees with five categories ($n = 15, 14, 11, 6, 5$) + unknown ($n = 5$).

2. *Financial and commercial dependence* (2 variables)

    (1) Distributors with seven categories ($n = 11, 5, 11, 9, 7, 11, 2$);

    (2) there is a publisher from another publishing company among the shareholders: yes ($n = 20$) or no ($n = 36$).

3. *Market share* (4 variables)

    (1) Commercial success based on two bestseller lists with five categories from "Sales1" to "Sales5" ($n = 28, 8, 8, 6, 6$);

    (2) publication of a book by one of the six main national prize winners (Goncourt, Femina, and so on): yes ($n = 13$) or no ($n = 43$);

    (3) publication of a book by a prize jury member: yes ($n = 12$) or no ($n = 44$);

    (4) financial subsidies from a ministry (Culture or Foreign Affairs) with five categories from "Sub1" to "Sub5" ($n = 25, 16, 6, 5, 4$).

4. *"Symbolic capital"* (4 variables)

    (1) Founding date with four categories: 1708–1945 ($n = 19$), 1946–75 ($n = 11$), 1976–1989 ($n = 17$), 1990–1995 ($n = 9$);

(2) "Jurt index" based on citations in history of literature textbooks, dictionaries, etc., with three categories: Jurt1 ($n = 44$), Jurt2 ($n = 7$), Jurt3 ($n = 5$);

(3) publication of a book by a French Nobel prize winner: yes ($n = 10$) or no ($n = 46$);

(4) location of company head office with five categories: three areas of Paris ($n = 29, 4, 9$), in the provinces ($n = 9$), and outside France ($n = 5$).

5. *Foreign literature* (3 variables)

(1) Percentage of books translated: four categories ($n = 17, 12, 16, 9$) + unknown ($n = 2$);

(2) publication of a book by a foreign Nobel prize winner: yes ($n = 14$) or no ($n = 42$);

(3) main translation languages during the study period with six categories: English only ($n = 9$), English and Western European languages ($n = 7$), English and other languages ($n = 16$), languages other than English ($n = 9$), none ($n = 8$), unclassifiable ($n = 7$).

A specific MCA (see Section 3.3, p. 61) was done by treating six categories as passive, namely, the four "unknown" categories, the "unclassifiable" one, and the one corresponding to a small distributor. The data correspond to $n = 56$ publishing companies and $Q = 16$ variables with $K' = 59$ active categories. The dimensionality of the clouds is therefore equal to $59 - (16 - 6) = 49$.

The contributions of the five headings are 22%, 14%, 23%, 23%, and 19%, respectively. They are almost of the same order of magnitude.

The first six eigenvalues are 0.4839, 0.2190, 0.1769, 0.1576, 0.1443, 0.1405. The modified rates are 0.693, 0.101, 0.056. The cumulated modified rate associated with the first three axes is 0.85. The first three axes are interpreted.

Interpretation of axes

• *Axis 1* ($\lambda_1 = 0.484$). The variables that contribute the most to this axis are the variables relating to *financial status*, *market share*, and *symbolic capital*. More precisely, the variables are the following ones:

• size index (contribution to axis 1: Ctr = 9.3%) and number of staff (Ctr = 9.1%);

- ministry subsidies (Ctr = 9.4%), publication of a book by a national prize winner (Ctr = 7.4%) and by a prize jury member (Ctr = 7.6%);

- founding date (Ctr = 7.9%), Jurt index (Ctr = 8.0%), and French Nobel prize winner (Ctr = 5.3%).

Together, the 25 categories selected for interpreting axis 1 (see Figure 6.1) contribute 79% to the variance of axis 1.

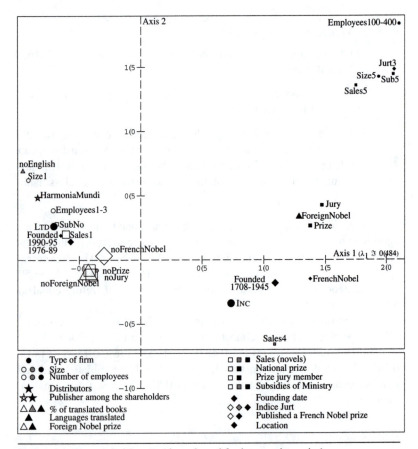

Figure 6.1 Plane 1-2: 25 categories selected for interpreting axis 1.

In Figure 6.2, from right to left the companies are ordered from the largest and oldest ones, which have a strong financial base and a high symbolic capital (Albin Michel, Flammarion, Gallimard, and Seuil), to the smallest ones, which are more recent and have fewer financial resources and less symbolic capital (e.g., Chambon, Climats, and Losfeld).

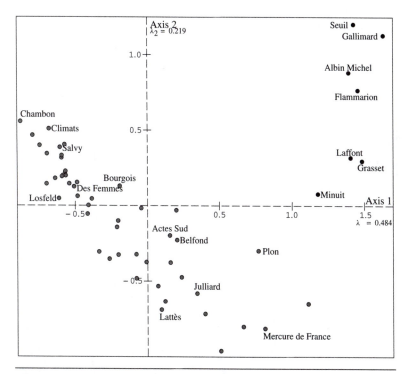

Figure 6.2 Cloud of 56 publishing companies in plane 1-2 (only the names of the companies mentioned in the text are shown).

• *Axis 2* ($\lambda_2 = 0.219$). The 22 categories selected for interpreting axis 2 contribute 80% to the variance of the axis. The variables that contribute most to the axis are the size index and the number of employees (Figure 6.3, p. 96), showing an opposition between (top) small and large size, no publishers as shareholders, no distributors and (bottom) medium size, one publisher among shareholders, Hachette and CDE[1] distributors.

The second axis distinguishes the publishers according to the capital structure: Independent publishers, either large (Flammarion, etc.) or small (e.g., Chambon, Des Femmes, or Salvy), are opposed to the subsidiaries of conglomerates (e.g., Lattès, Plon, or Mercure de France) that rely on other companies to distribute their publications (Figure 6.2).

---

[1] Centre de Diffusion de l'Édition.

96

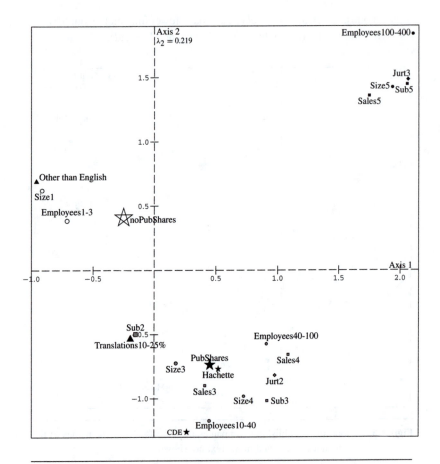

Figure 6.3 Plane 1-2: 22 categories selected for interpreting axis 2.

• *Axis 3* ($\lambda_3 = 0.177$). Axis 3 mainly opposes the publishers who, during the period, did not publish any (or very few) translations (e.g., Minuit or Mercure de France) to those who translated many books, mainly from English (e.g., Belfond, Bourgois, Actes Sud, or Salvy).

• *Class of seven major publishing companies*

In plane 1-2 (Figure 6.2, p. 95), seven publishers (black circles) are distinct from and opposed to the others (gray circles).

To characterize the group of these seven publishers, the relative frequency of each active category for the group was compared descriptively with that for the set of 56 publishers, taken as a reference frequency. Then, for the categories with large deviations, that is, greater than 10% (in absolute value), the hypergeometric test of typicality for frequency was performed (see Rouanet, 1998 et al., p. 102). If we retain the categories for which the deviations are descriptively large and statistically significant[2] (safety rule), this group can be characterized as follows.

They have the legal status of being incorporated companies and they are large companies (Size5, more than 100 employees); they have a large market share (Sales5, Sub5, publication of books by a national prize winner and by a prize jury member); their symbolic capital is high (Jurt3, founding date before 1946, publication of a French Nobel prize winner); they publish little foreign literature (less than 10%), but all of them have published a foreign Nobel prize winner.

The Bourdieu paper (1999) gives the results of and comments on a Euclidean clustering (ascending hierarchical clustering of a cloud of points according to the variance index) of the 56 publishing companies. The cluster of the 7 major publishing houses is constituted as early as the first dichotomy, which clearly demonstrates that these 7 publishers differ from the other 49. This cluster is only broken up at the seventh dichotomy, which shows its strong homogeneity.

6.2 The Norwegian Field of Power

Hereafter is sketched out the paper about the Norwegian elite by Hjell-brekke et al. (2007). The social structure of elites is analyzed as a *field of power* in Bourdieu's sense: a multidimensional space where agents compete together with various social resources. The construction of the space is based on Bourdieu's frame model of capitals: economic, social, and cultural capitals.

Three main questions are addressed: (1) What are the characteristics of the different dimensions of the field of power in terms of capitals? (2) What fractions of this field are the most open with respect to social mobility? (3) Are there particularly homogeneous fractions with respect to capital profiles?

Data Set and Coding

The data set is based on institutional criteria. It concerns 1 710 persons holding positions in the following institutions: business (348), cultural institutions (143), political system (190), police (78), justice system (60),

---

[2] $p < .025$, one-sided.

research and higher education (146), central administration (197), defense (68), church (107), cooperatives (42), media (116), organizations (215).

The sources of the data are public registers (income, property, and educational levels), and the Norwegian Power and Democracy Survey on Norwegian elites (2000). On the basis of the raw data, an important phase of coding was necessary to construct the relevant indicators of capital. Finally, we construct 31 questions, grouped under six headings, that constitute the active questions.

1. *Economic capital* (3 variables). Personal income, income on capital, registered property. Taking the first and third quartiles as indicative cutting values, these variables were recoded into 3 categories (low, medium, high).

2. *Personal educational capital* (3 variables). Educational level (6 categories), studies abroad (1 year, ≥ 2 years, no), worked abroad (yes, no).

3. *Inherited educational capital* (2 variables). Father's and partner's educational levels (5 categories).

4. *Inherited social capital* (5 variables). Five binary variables constructed from information on the parents' board memberships, coded yes (one or both parents) or no (neither parent).

5. *Personal social capital* (8 variables). Eight binary variables constructed from the information on respondent's board memberships.

6. *Professional experience* (10 variables). Ten binary variables constructed on whether or not the respondent has spent part of his/her career in 10 specific sectors.

Basic Results

The data set is gendered (85% are men). Age ranges from 28 to 76 (average 51.7 years, standard deviation 7.9). The position holders are well educated (62% have at least 5–6 years of university); their incomes and their inherited educational and social capitals are well above national average.

There are few missing data ("no information" categories); they concern the three economic capital variables and the three educational level variables. Moreover, the frequencies of these six categories are low (at most 15 individuals). These six categories are put as passive ones, thus a specific MCA was performed with 1,710 individuals and 77 active categories. Note that the contributions of the six headings to the total variance are of the same order of magnitude. Three axes were interpreted, whose variances are $\lambda_1 = 0.108$, $\lambda_2 = 0.082$, $\lambda_3 = 0.066$. The cumulated modified rate of the first three axes is equal to 0.75.

Interpretation of Axes

For the interpretation of an axis, the categories that have contributions greater than the average contribution ($100/77 = 1.3\%$) are selected. For better accounting for the questions with two categories, this basic criterion was lowered to 1.2%.

• *Axis 1* ($\lambda_1 = 0.108$): There are 19 categories that meet the criterion, to which we add the category (Income $\leq$421) with contribution 1.1% (near criterion) and close to category (Income 422–784) on axis 1. Together, they contribute 85.3% to the variance of axis. These 20 categories are depicted in Figure 6.4.

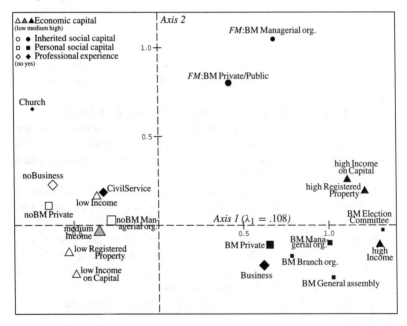

Figure 6.4 Plane 1-2. Interpretation of axis 1: 20 categories most contributing to axis. Abbreviations: *FM* = Father/Mother, BM = Board Member. The sizes of markers are proportional to the frequencies of categories.

On the left of Figure 6.4 (p. 99), the categories indicate low volume of economic capital, no business experience, no board membership of private business corporations, and no board membership of organizations; they also indicate experience in the Church and the Civil Service. *On the right*, the categories indicate high volume of economic capital, and a high degree of familiarity with "the business world" and economic executive power.

To sum up, the first axis is an axis of *economic capital*; it separates lower and higher volumes of economic capital assets.

• *Axis 2* ($\lambda_2 = 0.082$): The second axis is an axis of personal and inherited educational capital, combined with personal and inherited social capital, that is, an *axis of field seniority* (+ at the top, − at the bottom).

• *Axis 3* ($\lambda_3 = 0.066$): The third axis is an axis opposing *social capital assets and experience* in organizations, trade unions, the media, and politics, to *economic capital with experience* in justice; this axis also opposes lower educational levels to higher ones.

Structured Data Analysis

Taking the position variable as a structuring factor, for each of the 48 positions, we consider the subcloud of individuals who share this position, and we construct the 48 mean points of these subclouds, shown in Figure 6.5 (p. 101) in plane 1-2.

Moving from right to left, we find private and then public business positions, then organizational positions, followed by politicians. Moving from bottom to top, we find politicians, then civil servants and cultural positions, followed by leading positions in university and research, and then by leading positions in the Church.

In what follows, we focus on the following two subclouds: members of Parliament ($n = 138$) and public justice positions ($n = 60$), summarized by concentration ellipses.

In plane 1-2 (Figure 6.6), the two ellipses are on the side of low economic capital (axis 1). They show a larger dispersion along axis 2 (axis of field seniority) than along axis 1 (axis of economic capital); in each group, there are individual differences according to inherited social and educational capital, which is lower for the Parliament group than for the justice one.

In plane 2-3 (Figure 6.7, p. 102), the political ellipse is well separated from the justice one. The justice positions are identified as a homogeneous group with experience in justice (axis 3). This result suggests that it is difficult to gain access to the justice group; whereas for the Parliament group, there is experience in politics, but there are also relations with the media, organizations, trade unions, and so on.

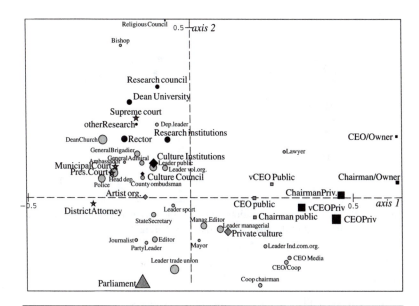

Figure 6.5 Cloud of individuals: The 45 mean points associated with positions divided in seven groups identified by different symbols, in plane 1-2.

Public business (▢), Private business (▮), Public culture (◆), Private culture (◇), Parliament (△), Justice (☆), University & Research (●). Other positions are written in smaller size letters and designated by (○).

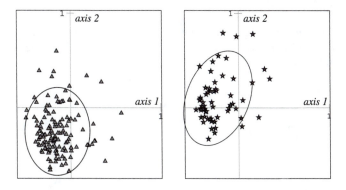

Figure 6.6 Plane 1-2. Concentration ellipses of the Parliament subcloud (*n* = 138, left) and of the Justice subcloud (*n* = 60, right).

102

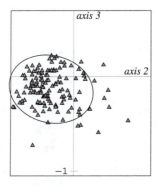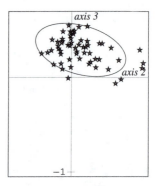

Figure 6.7 Plane 2-3. Concentration ellipses of the Parliament subcloud ($n = 138$, left) and of the Justice subcloud ($n = 60$, right).

Conclusions

The analysis leads to answering the three questions:

1. The Norwegian field of power can be described by three principal dimensions: an economic capital axis, an educational and social capital axis, and an axis separating the justice positions from positions in culture, organizations, and politics.

2. There is a distinct opposition between the "newcomers" and the "established"; the political positions are the most accessible ones, whereas the positions in research/university and in the Church are the least accessible ones.

3. The most homogeneous group is that of justice positions, although opposition between "newcomers" and "established" can be seen in this group.

APPENDIX

Symbol Index

Ctr_k contribution of category k

Ctr_q contribution of question q

d_{obs} observed effect

δ_{ik} disjunctive table of 0 and 1

η^2 correlation ratio

f_k relative frequency of category k

G mean point of cloud

I set of n individuals $i \in I$

I_k subset of n_k individuals who have chosen k

K overall set of categories

K_i response pattern of individual i

K_q set of response categories of question q

L dimensionality of cloud

ℓ ($\ell = 1, \ldots L$) enumeration index

λ_ℓ eigenvalue *or* variance of axis ℓ

$\mathbf{M}^i$ individual point

$\mathbf{M}^k$ category point

$\overline{\mathbf{M}}^k$ category mean point

n total number of individuals

n_k number of individuals who have chosen category k

$n_{kk'}$ number of individuals who have chosen both categories k and k'

$\tilde{n}$ weight of deviation

Φ^2 mean square contingency coefficient

p_k relative weight of category point $\mathbf{M}^k$

Q set of questions $q \in Q$

V_{cloud} variance of cloud

$v_{q\ell}$ variance of principal coordinates of category points for question q on axis ℓ

y_ℓ^i coordinate of individual point $\mathbf{M}^i$ relative to axis ℓ

y_ℓ^k coordinate of category point $\mathbf{M}^k$ relative to axis ℓ

$\overline{y}_\ell^k$ coordinate of category mean point $\overline{\mathbf{M}}^k$ relative to axis ℓ

ξ_ℓ singular value

z_{obs} observed value of test statistic Z

Abbreviations

AHC   Ascending Hierarchical Clustering

CA   Correspondence Analysis

CSA   Class Specific Analysis

GDA   Geometric Data Analysis

IDA   Inductive Data Analysis

MCA   Multiple Correspondence Analysis

PCA   Principal Component Analysis

SVD   Singular Value Decomposition

Matrix Formulas

We will express the computation procedures in matrix notation, used as a stenography.[1] It is useful for writing computer programs. Standard notation

---

[1] This section is not necessary for the rest of the book.

for matrices will be used, namely, bold uppercase letters in the general case, bold lowercase letters for column-vectors, and *prime symbol* (′) for transposition.

- $\mathbf{I}_I$ and $\mathbf{I}_K$ denote the $I \times I$ and $K \times K$ identity matrices, $\mathbf{e}_K$ the K column-vector of 1, and $\mathbf{e}_I$ the I column-vector of 1;

- $\mathbf{N}_K$ denotes the $K \times K$ diagonal matrix of n_k;

- $\mathbf{Z}$ denotes the $I \times K$ matrix with entries δ_{ik} (disjunctive table), such that $\mathbf{Z}\mathbf{e}_K = Q\mathbf{e}_I$ and $\mathbf{Z}'\mathbf{e}_I = \mathbf{N}_K\mathbf{e}_K$;

- $\mathbf{Z}_0 = \mathbf{Z} - \frac{1}{n}\,\mathbf{e}_I\mathbf{e}_I'\mathbf{Z}$ denotes the $I \times K$ matrix with entries $\delta_{ik} - (n_k/n)$;

- $\mathbf{y}_K$ denotes the K column-vector and $\mathbf{Y}_K$ the $K \times L$ matrix of the principal coordinates of the K category points;

- $\mathbf{y}_I$ denotes the I column-vector and $\mathbf{Y}_I$ the $I \times L$ matrix of the principal coordinates of the I individual points.

We will present in detail the computation procedures for regular MCA, and we will only give the formulas for the specific MCA and CSA.

Regular MCA

Let us write the *transition formulas* (p. 41) in terms of δ_{ik} (p. 36):

$$y^i = \frac{1}{\sqrt{\lambda}} \sum_k \delta_{ik} y^k / Q \quad \text{and} \quad y^k = \frac{1}{\sqrt{\lambda}} \sum_i \delta_{ik} y^i / n_k.$$

In matrix notation:

1) $\mathbf{y}_I = \frac{1}{\sqrt{\lambda}} \frac{1}{Q} \mathbf{Z}\mathbf{y}_K$

2) $\mathbf{y}_K = \frac{1}{\sqrt{\lambda}} \mathbf{N}_K^{-1}\mathbf{Z}'\mathbf{y}_I$

with $\frac{1}{n}\mathbf{y}_I'\,\mathbf{y}_I = \lambda = \frac{1}{nQ}\mathbf{y}_K'\mathbf{N}_K\,\mathbf{y}_K.$

Notice that, since the principal variables are centered, we can replace δ_{ik} by $\delta_{ik} - (n_k/n)$ in the formulas, that is, $\mathbf{Z}$ by $\mathbf{Z}_0$.

- *Singular Value Decomposition (SVD).*

Let $\xi = \sqrt{\lambda}$ (singular value),

$$\mathbf{u} = \frac{1}{\sqrt{n}} \frac{1}{\xi}\mathbf{y}_I, \quad \mathbf{v} = \frac{1}{\sqrt{nQ}} \frac{1}{\xi}\mathbf{N}_K^{1/2}\mathbf{y}_K,$$

with $\mathbf{u}'\mathbf{u} = 1 = \mathbf{v}'\mathbf{v}$. Replacing $\mathbf{y}_K$ and $\mathbf{y}_I$ by their expressions in terms of $\mathbf{u}$ and $\mathbf{v}$, one gets, after simplification, the two equations:

$$\frac{1}{\sqrt{Q}} \, \mathbf{Z}_0 \mathbf{N}_K^{-1/2} \mathbf{v} = \xi \mathbf{u} \quad \text{and} \quad \frac{1}{\sqrt{Q}} \, \mathbf{N}_K^{-1/2} \mathbf{Z}_0' \mathbf{u} = \xi \mathbf{v}.$$

$(\mathbf{u}, \mathbf{v}, \xi)$ will be determined by the SVD of the $I \times K$ matrix $\mathbf{H} = \mathbf{Z}_0 \mathbf{N}_K^{-1/2}/\sqrt{Q}$.

The SVD yields the matrices Ξ (L-diagonal), $\mathbf{U}$ ($I \times L$), and $\mathbf{V}$ ($K \times L$), such that $\mathbf{H} = \mathbf{U}\Xi\mathbf{V}'$, with $\mathbf{U}'\mathbf{U} = \mathbf{I}_I$, $\mathbf{V}'\mathbf{V} = \mathbf{I}_K$.

The L principal coordinates of the I individual points and that of K category points are then:

$$\mathbf{Y}_I = \sqrt{n} \, \mathbf{U}\Xi \quad \text{and} \quad \mathbf{Y}_K = \sqrt{nQ} \, \mathbf{N}_K^{-1/2} \mathbf{V}\Xi.$$

Remark. The column-vectors $\mathbf{e}_I$ and $\mathbf{N}_K^{1/2}\mathbf{e}_K$ are eigenvectors of $\mathbf{H}$ associated with $\xi_0 = 0$.

- *Diagonalization procedure*

The column-vector $\mathbf{v}$ is also an eigenvector of the $K \times K$ symmetric matrix $\mathbf{S} = \mathbf{H}'\mathbf{H}$ associated with the eigenvalue $\lambda = \xi^2$. Therefore, if we let $\mathbf{B} = \mathbf{Z}'\mathbf{Z}$ be the Burt matrix (defined on p. 43) and $\mathbf{B}_0 = \mathbf{B} - \frac{1}{n}\mathbf{N}_K\mathbf{e}_K\mathbf{e}_K'\mathbf{N}_K$ be the matrix with entries $n_{kk'} - (n_k n_{k'}/n)$, we have $\mathbf{S} = \mathbf{N}_K^{-1/2}\mathbf{B}_0\,\mathbf{N}_K^{-1/2}$ and $\mathbf{Sv} = \lambda\,\mathbf{v}$. The diagonalization of the matrix $\mathbf{S}$ yields the matrices Λ (L-diagonal) and $\mathbf{V}$ as above with $\mathbf{S} = \mathbf{V}\Lambda\mathbf{V}'$.

The coordinates of category points are $\mathbf{Y}_K$; as above, those of individual points can be calculated using the disjunctive table:

$$\mathbf{Y}_I = \sqrt{n} \, \mathbf{Z}\mathbf{N}_K^{-1/2}\mathbf{V}/\sqrt{Q}.$$

Specific MCA

The matrices to be analyzed will be submatrices of the initial ones, using only K' (active categories). We denote by $\widetilde{\mathbf{Z}}_0$ and $\widetilde{\mathbf{H}}_0$ the $I \times K'$ submatrices of $\mathbf{Z}_0$ and $\mathbf{H}_0$, respectively, $\mathbf{N}_{K'}$ the submatrix of $\mathbf{N}_K$, and $\widetilde{\mathbf{y}}_{K'}$ and $\widetilde{\mathbf{y}}_I$ the column-vectors of the specific coordinates, respectively.

In matrix notation, the *transition equations* of page 63 are as follows:

1) $\widetilde{\mathbf{y}}_I = \frac{1}{\sqrt{\mu}} \frac{1}{Q} \widetilde{\mathbf{Z}}_0 \widetilde{\mathbf{y}}_{K'}$

2) $\widetilde{\mathbf{y}}_{K'} = \frac{1}{\sqrt{\mu}} \mathbf{N}_{K'}^{-1}\widetilde{\mathbf{Z}}_0'\widetilde{\mathbf{y}}_I$

with $\frac{1}{n}\widetilde{\mathbf{y}}_I'\widetilde{\mathbf{y}}_I = \mu = \frac{1}{nQ}\widetilde{\mathbf{y}}_{K'}'\mathbf{N}_{K'}\widetilde{\mathbf{y}}_{K'}.$

- *Singular value decomposition*

Let $\mathbf{M}$ be the L-diagonal matrix of eigenvalues μ and $\Gamma = \mathbf{M}^{1/2}$ that of singular values $\gamma = \sqrt{\mu}$. Specific MCA consists in the SVD of the $I \times K'$

matrix $\tilde{\mathbf{H}}_0 = \frac{1}{\sqrt{Q}} \tilde{\mathbf{Z}}_0 \mathbf{N}_{K'}^{-1/2}$, that yields $\tilde{\mathbf{H}}_0 = \tilde{\mathbf{U}} \Gamma \tilde{\mathbf{V}}'$, with $\tilde{\mathbf{U}}' \tilde{\mathbf{U}} = \mathbf{I}_I$ and $\tilde{\mathbf{V}}' \tilde{\mathbf{V}} = \mathbf{I}_{K'}$.

The L principal coordinates $\tilde{\mathbf{Y}}_I$ of the I individual points and the L principal coordinates of $\tilde{\mathbf{Y}}_{K'}$ of the K' category points are such that:

$$\tilde{\mathbf{Y}}_I = \sqrt{n}\, \tilde{\mathbf{U}} \Gamma \quad \text{and} \quad \tilde{\mathbf{Y}}_{K'} = \sqrt{nQ}\, \mathbf{N}_{K'}^{-1/2} \tilde{\mathbf{V}} \Gamma.$$

- *Diagonalization procedure*

The diagonalization of the $K' \times K'$ matrix $\tilde{\mathbf{S}} = \tilde{\mathbf{H}}_0' \tilde{\mathbf{H}}_0 = \mathbf{N}_{K'}^{-1/2} \tilde{\mathbf{B}}_0 \, \mathbf{N}_{K'}^{-1/2}$ yields $\tilde{\mathbf{S}} = \tilde{\mathbf{V}} \mathbf{M} \tilde{\mathbf{V}}'$, with $\tilde{\mathbf{V}}' \tilde{\mathbf{V}} = \mathbf{I}_{K'}$. The principal coordinates of the K' category points are then $\tilde{\mathbf{Y}}_{K'}$, as above; that of the I individual points are $\tilde{\mathbf{Y}}_I = \sqrt{n}\, \tilde{\mathbf{Z}}_0 \mathbf{N}_{K'}^{-1/2} \tilde{\mathbf{V}} / \sqrt{Q}$.

Class Specific Analysis

Keeping the notation $\mathbf{N}_K$ for the K-diagonal matrix of the absolute frequencies N_k of categories in the set I of the N individuals, we denote:

- $\widehat{\mathbf{N}}_K$ as the K-diagonal matrix of the absolute frequencies n_k of categories in the subset I' of the n individuals;

- $\widehat{\mathbf{Z}}$ as the $I' \times K$ submatrix of the $I \times K$ matrix $\mathbf{Z}$;

- $\widehat{\mathbf{Z}}_0 = \widehat{\mathbf{Z}} - \frac{1}{n} \mathbf{e}_{I'} \mathbf{e}_K' \widehat{\mathbf{N}}_K$ as the $I' \times K$ matrix with entries $\delta_{ik} - (n_k/n)$;

- $\widehat{\mathbf{y}}_K$ and $\widehat{\mathbf{y}}_{I'}$ as the column-vectors of the specific coordinates of the K category points and of the I' individual points.

The transition formulas of page 65 can thus be written:

1) $\widehat{\mathbf{y}}_{I'} = \frac{1}{\sqrt{\mu}} \frac{1}{Q} \widehat{\mathbf{Z}}_0 \widehat{\mathbf{y}}_K$

2) $\widehat{\mathbf{y}}_K = \frac{1}{\sqrt{\mu}} N \mathbf{N}_K^{-1} \widehat{\mathbf{Z}}_0' \widehat{\mathbf{y}}_{I'}$

with $\frac{1}{n} \widehat{\mathbf{y}}_{I'}' \widehat{\mathbf{y}}_{I'} = \mu = \frac{1}{NQ} \widehat{\mathbf{y}}_K' \mathbf{N}_K \widehat{\mathbf{y}}_K$.

- *Singular value decomposition*

CSA consists in the SVD of the $I' \times K$ matrix

$$\widehat{\mathbf{H}} = \frac{1}{\sqrt{Q}} \sqrt{\frac{N}{n}}\, \widehat{\mathbf{Z}}_0 \mathbf{N}_K^{-1/2}.$$

Hence the matrices Γ (L-diagonal), $\widehat{\mathbf{U}}$ ($I' \times L$), and $\widehat{\mathbf{V}}$ ($K \times L$), such that $\widehat{\mathbf{H}} = \widehat{\mathbf{U}} \Gamma \widehat{\mathbf{V}}'$, with $\widehat{\mathbf{U}}' \widehat{\mathbf{U}} = \mathbf{I}_{I'}$ and $\widehat{\mathbf{V}}' \widehat{\mathbf{V}} = \mathbf{I}_K$.

The L principal coordinates of the I' individual points and of the K category points are then:

$$\widehat{\mathbf{Y}}_{I'} = \sqrt{n}\, \widehat{\mathbf{U}} \Gamma \quad \text{and} \quad \widehat{\mathbf{Y}}_K = \sqrt{QN}\, \mathbf{N}_K^{-1/2} \widehat{\mathbf{V}} \Gamma.$$

- *Diagonalization procedure*

Let $\widehat{\mathbf{B}} = \widehat{\mathbf{Z}}'\widehat{\mathbf{Z}}$ be the Burt matrix of the subset I' (with entries $n_{kk'}$) and $\widehat{\mathbf{B}}_0 = \widehat{\mathbf{B}} - \frac{1}{n}\widehat{\mathbf{N}}_K \mathbf{e}_K \mathbf{e}'_K \widehat{\mathbf{N}}_K$ be the matrix with entries $n_{kk'} - (n_k\, n_{k'}/n)$. The diagonalization of the matrix $\widehat{\mathbf{S}} = \widehat{\mathbf{H}}'\widehat{\mathbf{H}} = \frac{1}{Q}\frac{N}{n}\mathbf{N}_K^{-1/2}\widehat{\mathbf{B}}_0\mathbf{N}_K^{-1/2}$ yields the matrices $\widehat{\mathbf{V}}$ and Γ with $\widehat{\mathbf{S}} = \widehat{\mathbf{V}}\Gamma\widehat{\mathbf{V}}'$. Hence $\widehat{\mathbf{Y}}_K$, as above, and, using the disjunctive table $\widehat{\mathbf{Z}}_0$, $\widehat{\mathbf{Y}}_{I'} = (N/\sqrt{Q})\,\widehat{\mathbf{Z}}_0\mathbf{N}_K^{-1/2}\widehat{\mathbf{V}}$.

Software for MCA

All numerical results for (regular and specific) MCA can be obtained from the formulas of Appendix (p. 103), using a language with a library that includes good procedures for singular value decomposition or symmetric matrix diagonalization such as R (or S+), C, Fortran, and so forth. After storing the coordinates of category points and of individual points, proceed to the graphical representation of clouds with appropriate software.

Standard packages may also be used, but the results of MCA provided by almost all of them, whether free or not, are often incomplete (not to say incorrect).[2]

Free software. We will cite R language packages and ADDAD software.

- In R (R Development Core Team, www.r-project.org), the mca() function provides the results of regular MCA. However, the implementation of this function is kept to a minimum: neither supplementary elements, nor recent developments. In the ca package, the mjca() function gives the regular MCA results including results about supplementary categories and some recent developments (see the appendix by Nenadić and Greenacre in Greenacre & Blasius, 2006). The FactoMineR package (developed by F. Husson, S. Lê, J. Josse, and J. Mazet, http://factominer.free.fr/) is easy to use. It contains most of the methods presented in this monograph including test-values and inertia ellipses.[3]

- ADDAD (available from the the first author's Web site) provides eigenvalues, coordinates, and contributions of both active and supplementary elements for regular and specific MCAs. The coordinates can be stored, which permits the construction of graphical representations of clouds with an appropriate interface.

---

[2] This survey has been made with the help of Philippe Bonnet (Université Paris Descartes), whom we gratefully thank.

[3] ca and FactoMineR packages are also described in the *Journal of Statistical Software*, Vol. 20, Issue 3 (May 2007) for ca and in Vol. 25, Issue 1 (March 2008) for FactoMineR.

Commercial packages. Most standard packages provide the basic numerical results of *regular MCA* (eigenvalues, coordinates, and contributions); yet the graphs are often imperfect, if not unreadable.

XLSTAT (www.xlstat.com),[4] SPSS (www.spss.com),[5] SAS/Stat (www.sas.com),[6] and STATA (www.stata.com)[7] make it possible to obtain not only the basic results but also those for supplementary elements. The coordinates of individuals (cases) can also be stored.

In any case, make sure that (a) the variances of principal variables (coordinates of categories and of individuals) are equal to the corresponding eigenvalues; (b) the scales of graphs are the same for abscissas and ordinates.

To perform MCA in a user-friendly way, we recommend the SPAD (release 7.0) software (www.spad.eu). The user can obtain eigenvalues, modified rates, coordinates, contributions, supplementary elements and test-values for both regular and specific MCAs. All results are returned in the Excel environment. This means that it is very easy to make additional computations on the results. Furthermore, the graphical module is very easy to use. It gives highly readable graphical representations of clouds of individuals and of categories, as well as of subclouds for interpreting axes, in an interactive way. It also permits users to represent subclouds with concentration and confidence ellipses.[8]

---

[4] Open XLSTAT and select "XLSTAT>Analyzing data>Multiple Correspondence Analysis" command.

[5] We do not recommend the use of this package to perform MCA since it yields imprecise results. The default convergence criterion (10^{-5}) must be lowered even for a very small data set. This can be done only by writing the SPSS syntax. Furthermore, to obtain the principal coordinates of individual points as well as of category points (with variances equal to eigenvalues, see p. 40) two analyses must be performed: one with the option "vprincipal," which yields the coordinates of category points, and one with the option "oprincipal," which yields those of individual points.

[6] Proceed to the analysis of the Individuals × Variables table using the "PROC CORRESP" without the option "MCA."

[7] In STATA (release 11), enter a data set (File>Open) and perform MCA (Statistics>Multivariate Analysis>Correspondence Analysis>Multiple correspondence Analysis (MCA)) selecting the options (indicator matrix approach) for the method and (principal) for the normalization. *Remark*: The sum of what they call "contr" (or "contrib") is not equal to 1000 (or 1); to obtain the genuine contributions of category points to an axis, as defined on p. 40 (Ctr), divide the "contr"s by their sum, that is, the square root of the eigenvalue.

[8] There is a plug-in for R in SPAD, thus allowing R scripts to be executed in SPAD project. It is then easy to modify SPAD bases or to create new ones with R. Plots generated by R scripts can be edited in SPAD interface.

On the first author's Web site the data set of the Taste Example, a guide for running MCA using SPAD and ADDAD, and information on other packages may be found, in addition to a .pdf file with *color versions* of many graphs.

REFERENCES

Benzécri, J.-P. (1969). Statistical analysis as a tool to make patterns emerge from data. In S. Watanabe (Ed.), *Methodologies of pattern recognition* (pp. 35–74). New York: Academic Press.

Benzécri, J.-P. (1982). *Histoire et Préhistoire de l'Analyse des Données*. Paris: Dunod.

Benzécri, J.-P. (1992). *Correspondence analysis handbook*. New York: Dekker. (Adapted from J.-P. Benzécri & F. Benzécri, 1984)

Benzécri, J.-P., et al. (1973). *L'Analyse des Données. Vol. 1: Taxinomie. Vol. 2: Analyse des correspondances* [Data analysis. Vol. 1: Taxinomy. Vol. 2: Correspondence analysis]. Paris: Dunod.

Bourdieu, P. (1979). *La Distinction: Critique Sociale du Jugement*. Paris: Editions de Minuit (English translation: *Distinction* (1984). Boston: Harvard University Press)

Bourdieu, P. (1999). Une révolution conservatrice dans l'édition. *Actes de la Recherche en Sciences Sociales, 126–127*, 3–28 (A conservative revolution in publishing. 2008. *Translation Studies, 1*, 123–153.)

Bourdieu P. (2001). *Science de la science et réflexivité. Cours du Collége de France 2000–2001*. Paris: Liber.

Bourdieu P. & Saint-Martin M. (1976). Anatomie du goût, *Acts de la Recherche en Sciences Sociales*, Vol. 5, 1–110.

Burt, C. (1950). The factorial analysis of qualitative data. *British Journal of Psychology, 3*, 166–185.

Chiche, J., Le Roux, B., Perrineau, P., & Rouanet, H. (2000). L'espace politique des électeurs français à la fin des années 1990 [The French electoral space at the end of the 1990s]. *Revue française de sciences politiques, 50*, 463–487.

Clausen, S. E. (1998). *Applied correspondence analysis: An introduction* (QASS Series). Thousand Oaks, CA: Sage.

Cramér, H. (1946). *Mathematical methods of statistics*. Princeton, NJ: Princeton University Press.

Edgington, E. S., & Onghena, P. (2007). *Randomization tests* (4th ed.). London: Chapman & Hall.

Fisher, R. A. (1940). The precision of discriminant functions. *Annals of Eugenics, 10*, 422–429.

Freedman, D., & Lane, D. (1983). A nonstochastic interpretation of reported significance levels. *Journal of Business and Economic Statistics, 1*, 292–298.

Gifi, A. (1990). *Nonlinear multivariate analysis*. Chichester, UK: Wiley. [Adapted from A. Gifi, 1981]

Greenacre, M. (1984). *Theory and applications of correspondence analysis*. London: Academic Press.

Greenacre, M. (1993). *Correspondence analysis in practice*. London: Academic Press.

Greenacre, M., & Blasius, J. (Eds.). (2006). *Multiple correspondence analysis and related methods*. London: Chapman & Hall.

Guttman, L. (1941). The quantification of a class of attributes: A theory and method of scale construction. In P. Horst (with collaboration of P. Wallin & L. Guttman) (Ed.), *The prediction of personal adjustment* (pp. 319–348). New York: Social Science Research Council.

Hayashi, C. (1952). On the prediction of phenomena from qualitative data and the quantification of qualitative data from the mathematico-statistical point of view. *Annals of the Institute of Statistical Mathematics, 3*(2).

Hjellbrekke, J., Le Roux, B., Korsnes, O., Lebaron, F., Rosenlund, L., & Rouanet, H. (2007). The Norwegian field of power anno 2000. *European Societies, 9*(2), 245–273.

Kendall, M. G., & Stuart, A. (1973–1984). *The advanced theory of statistics* (Vols. 1–3). London: Griffin.

Le Roux, B., & Rouanet, H. (2003). *Geometric analysis of individual differences in mathematical performance for EPGY students in the third grade*. Retrieved September 1, 2009, from http://epgy.stanford.edu/research/GeometricData Analysis.pdf

Le Roux, B., & Rouanet, H. (2004). *Geometric data analysis. From correspondence analysis to structured data analysis* (Foreword by P. Suppes). Dordrecht, the Netherlands: Kluwer–Springer.

Le Roux, B., Rouanet, H., Savage, M., & Warde, A. (2008). Class and cultural division in the UK. *Sociology, 42*, 1049–1071.

Lebart, L. (1975). L'orientation du dépouillement de certaines enquêtes par l'analyse des correspondances multiples [The orientation of the analysis of some surveys using multiple correspondence analysis]. *Consommation, 2*, 73–96.

Lebart, L., & Fénelon, J.-P. (1971). *Statistique et informatique appliquées* [Applied statistics and informatics]. Paris: Dunod.

Lebart, L., Morineau, A., & Warwick, K. M. (1984). *Multivariate descriptive statistical analysis: Correspondence analysis and related techniques for large matrices*. New York: Wiley.

Murtagh, F. (2005). *Correspondence analysis and data coding with Java and R*. London: Chapman & Hall.

Rouanet, H. (2006). The geometric analysis of structured Individuals × Variables tables. In M. Greenacre & J. Blasius (Eds.), *Multiple correspondence analysis and related methods* (pp. 137–159). London: Chapman & Hall.

112

Rouanet, H., Ackermann, W., & Le Roux, B. (2000). The geometric analysis of questionnaires: The lesson of Bourdieu's La Distinction. *Bulletin de Méthodologie Sociologique, 65,* 5–18. Retrieved September 1, 2009, from http://www .mi.parisdescartes.fr/~lerb/rouanet/recherche/publications/newless.html

Rouanet, H., Bernard, J.-M., Bert, M. C., Lecoutre, B., Lecoutre, M. P., & Le Roux, B. (1998). *New ways in statistical methodology: From significance tests to Bayesian methods.* Bern, Switzerland: Peter Lang.

Shepard, R. N. (1962). The analysis of proximities: Multidimensional scaling with an unknown distance function. *Psychometrika, 27,* 125–139, 219–246.

Weller, S. C., & Romney, A. K. (1990). *Metric scaling: Correspondence analysis.* Newbury Park, CA: Sage.

INDEX